50 Mexican Restaurant Food Recipes for Home

By: Kelly Johnson

Table of Contents

- Tacos al Pastor
- Chicken Enchiladas
- Beef Burritos
- Pork Carnitas
- Chimichangas
- Tamales
- Quesadillas
- Fish Tacos
- Huevos Rancheros
- Mexican Street Corn (Elote)
- Pozole
- Chicken Mole
- Chiles Rellenos
- Sopes
- Flautas
- Mexican Rice
- Refried Beans
- Guacamole
- Salsa Verde
- Pico de Gallo
- Ceviche
- Tostadas
- Albondigas (Mexican Meatballs)
- Queso Fundido
- Tamale Pie
- Enchilada Sauce
- Mexican Street Tacos
- Chilaquiles
- Carnitas Tacos
- Barbacoa Beef
- Margarita Chicken
- Cactus Salad (Nopales)

- Baked Mexican Chicken
- Mexican Stuffed Peppers
- Coconut Flan
- Tres Leches Cake
- Mexican Hot Chocolate
- Mexican Shrimp Cocktail
- Churros
- Spicy Black Beans
- Tortilla Soup
- Mexican Cornbread
- Salsa Roja
- Chicken Pozole
- El Pastor Marinade
- Taco Salad
- Huaraches
- Mexican Pizza
- Tinga de Pollo
- Puerco en Salsa Verde

Tacos al Pastor

Ingredients:

For the Marinade:

- 2 pounds pork shoulder, thinly sliced
- 1/4 cup achiote paste
- 1/4 cup white vinegar
- 1/2 cup orange juice
- 1/4 cup pineapple juice
- 2 cloves garlic, minced
- 1 tablespoon chili powder
- 1 teaspoon cumin
- 1 teaspoon dried oregano
- 1/2 teaspoon paprika
- 1/4 teaspoon ground cloves
- 1/4 teaspoon ground cinnamon
- Salt and pepper, to taste

For the Tacos:

- 12 small corn tortillas
- 1 small pineapple, peeled, cored, and sliced into rings
- 1 small onion, finely chopped
- 1/2 cup fresh cilantro, chopped
- Lime wedges
- Salsa (optional)

Instructions:

1. **Prepare the Marinade:**
    - In a bowl, combine achiote paste, vinegar, orange juice, pineapple juice, minced garlic, chili powder, cumin, oregano, paprika, cloves, cinnamon, salt, and pepper.
    - Mix well until the marinade is smooth.
2. **Marinate the Pork:**
    - Place the sliced pork in a large resealable plastic bag or a bowl.
    - Pour the marinade over the pork, making sure each slice is well-coated.
    - Seal the bag or cover the bowl and refrigerate for at least 4 hours, preferably overnight.
3. **Cook the Pork:**
    - Preheat a grill or a large skillet over medium-high heat.
    - Grill or cook the pork slices for about 3-4 minutes per side, or until cooked through and slightly charred.

- If using a grill, you can also grill the pineapple slices until caramelized and grill marks appear.
4. **Prepare the Tacos:**
    - Warm the tortillas on a grill or in a skillet.
    - Slice the cooked pork into small, bite-sized pieces.
    - Dice the grilled pineapple into small chunks.
5. **Assemble the Tacos:**
    - Place a few pieces of pork on each tortilla.
    - Top with pineapple chunks, chopped onion, and fresh cilantro.
    - Serve with lime wedges and salsa on the side if desired.

Enjoy your delicious Tacos al Pastor!

Chicken Enchiladas

Ingredients:

For the Enchiladas:

- 2 cups cooked, shredded chicken (from about 2 chicken breasts or thighs)
- 10-12 corn or flour tortillas
- 1 cup grated cheese (cheddar, Monterey Jack, or a blend)
- 1 small onion, finely chopped
- 2 cloves garlic, minced
- 1/2 cup sour cream (optional, for garnish)
- 1/4 cup fresh cilantro, chopped (optional, for garnish)

For the Enchilada Sauce:

- 2 tablespoons vegetable oil
- 1 small onion, finely chopped
- 2 cloves garlic, minced
- 1/4 cup chili powder
- 1 tablespoon ground cumin
- 1 tablespoon tomato paste
- 1 1/2 cups tomato sauce
- 1 cup chicken broth
- 1 teaspoon sugar
- Salt and pepper, to taste

Instructions:

1. **Prepare the Enchilada Sauce:**
    - Heat the vegetable oil in a medium saucepan over medium heat.
    - Add the chopped onion and cook until softened, about 5 minutes.
    - Stir in the minced garlic and cook for another minute.
    - Add the chili powder, cumin, and tomato paste. Cook for 1-2 minutes, stirring frequently.
    - Pour in the tomato sauce and chicken broth. Stir to combine.
    - Add the sugar, and season with salt and pepper to taste.
    - Bring the sauce to a simmer, then reduce heat and let it cook for about 10-15 minutes, until slightly thickened.
2. **Prepare the Filling:**
    - In a large bowl, combine the shredded chicken with 1/2 cup of the prepared enchilada sauce and half of the grated cheese. Mix well.
3. **Assemble the Enchiladas:**
    - Preheat your oven to 375°F (190°C).

- Lightly grease a 9x13-inch baking dish.
- Warm the tortillas in a dry skillet or microwave to make them more pliable.
- Spread a thin layer of enchilada sauce in the bottom of the baking dish.
- For each tortilla, spoon about 2-3 tablespoons of the chicken mixture down the center. Roll up the tortilla and place it seam-side down in the baking dish.
- Repeat with the remaining tortillas and chicken mixture.
- Once all the tortillas are in the dish, pour the remaining enchilada sauce over the top, making sure to cover all the tortillas.
- Sprinkle the remaining cheese over the top.

4. **Bake:**
   - Cover the baking dish with aluminum foil and bake in the preheated oven for 20 minutes.
   - Remove the foil and bake for an additional 10 minutes, or until the cheese is melted and bubbly and the enchiladas are heated through.

5. **Garnish and Serve:**
   - Allow the enchiladas to cool for a few minutes before serving.
   - Garnish with sour cream and fresh cilantro if desired.

Enjoy your homemade Chicken Enchiladas!

Beef Burritos

Ingredients:

For the Beef Filling:

- 1 lb ground beef
- 1 small onion, finely chopped
- 2 cloves garlic, minced
- 1 bell pepper, finely chopped (optional)
- 1 packet (1 oz) taco seasoning mix (or use homemade seasoning)
- 1/2 cup tomato sauce
- 1/2 cup beef broth
- 1 cup cooked rice
- 1 cup canned black beans, drained and rinsed (optional)
- 1 cup shredded cheese (cheddar, Monterey Jack, or a blend)

For Assembly:

- 6-8 large flour tortillas
- 1 cup sour cream (optional)
- 1 cup salsa (optional)
- 1/2 cup chopped fresh cilantro (optional)

Instructions:

1. **Prepare the Beef Filling:**
   - In a large skillet, cook the ground beef over medium-high heat until browned, breaking it up with a spoon as it cooks.
   - Drain excess fat if needed.
   - Add the chopped onion and cook for about 5 minutes, until softened.
   - Stir in the minced garlic and bell pepper (if using), and cook for another 2 minutes.
   - Add the taco seasoning mix, tomato sauce, and beef broth. Stir to combine.
   - Reduce heat and simmer for 10-15 minutes, until the mixture thickens and flavors meld together.
   - Stir in the cooked rice and black beans (if using), and cook for an additional 5 minutes.
2. **Assemble the Burritos:**
   - Warm the tortillas in a dry skillet or microwave to make them more pliable.
   - Lay a tortilla flat on a plate or work surface.
   - Spoon a portion of the beef filling down the center of the tortilla.
   - Top with shredded cheese.
   - Fold in the sides of the tortilla and roll it up from the bottom to encase the filling.

- Repeat with the remaining tortillas and filling.
3. **Optional: Heat the Burritos:**
    - For extra flavor and to melt the cheese, you can heat the assembled burritos.
    - Heat a large skillet over medium heat. Place the burritos seam-side down and cook for about 2-3 minutes on each side, until golden brown and the cheese is melted.
4. **Serve:**
    - Serve the burritos with optional sides like sour cream, salsa, and chopped fresh cilantro.

Enjoy your Beef Burritos!

Pork Carnitas

Ingredients:

- 3-4 lbs pork shoulder (also known as pork butt), trimmed and cut into large chunks
- 1 large onion, chopped
- 4 cloves garlic, minced
- 1 orange, juiced (reserve the spent halves)
- 1 lime, juiced
- 1 tablespoon chili powder
- 1 tablespoon ground cumin
- 1 teaspoon paprika
- 1 teaspoon dried oregano
- 1/2 teaspoon ground coriander
- 1/2 teaspoon ground black pepper
- 1-2 bay leaves
- 1-2 cups chicken or beef broth
- 2 tablespoons vegetable oil
- Salt, to taste

Instructions:

1. **Prepare the Pork:**
    - Pat the pork shoulder chunks dry with paper towels.
    - In a large bowl, combine chili powder, cumin, paprika, oregano, coriander, black pepper, and salt. Rub this spice mixture all over the pork chunks.
2. **Sear the Pork:**
    - Heat vegetable oil in a large Dutch oven or heavy-bottomed pot over medium-high heat.
    - Sear the pork chunks in batches until browned on all sides, about 3-4 minutes per side. Remove the pork and set aside.
3. **Cook the Carnitas:**
    - In the same pot, add chopped onion and cook until softened, about 5 minutes.
    - Add minced garlic and cook for another minute.
    - Return the seared pork to the pot.
    - Pour in the orange juice, lime juice, and enough chicken or beef broth to just cover the meat. Place the spent orange halves and bay leaves in the pot.
    - Bring to a simmer.
4. **Simmer:**
    - Cover the pot and reduce the heat to low.
    - Simmer gently for about 2.5 to 3 hours, or until the pork is very tender and shreds easily with a fork. Stir occasionally and check the liquid level, adding more broth if necessary.

5. **Crisp the Carnitas:**
    - Once the pork is tender, remove it from the pot and shred it with two forks.
    - Preheat your oven's broiler to high or heat a large skillet over medium-high heat.
    - Spread the shredded pork on a baking sheet and drizzle a little of the cooking liquid over it.
    - Broil in the oven or cook in the skillet, stirring occasionally, until the edges of the pork become crispy and caramelized, about 5-10 minutes.
6. **Serve:**
    - Serve the crispy carnitas with warm tortillas and your favorite toppings, such as salsa, guacamole, chopped onions, cilantro, and lime wedges.

Enjoy your flavorful and crispy Pork Carnitas!

Chimichangas

Ingredients:

For the Filling:

- 1 lb ground beef (or shredded chicken for variation)
- 1 small onion, finely chopped
- 2 cloves garlic, minced
- 1 bell pepper, finely chopped (optional)
- 1 packet (1 oz) taco seasoning mix (or homemade seasoning)
- 1/2 cup tomato sauce
- 1/2 cup canned black beans, drained and rinsed (optional)
- 1 cup cooked rice
- 1 cup shredded cheese (cheddar, Monterey Jack, or a blend)
- Salt and pepper, to taste

For Assembly:

- 8 large flour tortillas
- Vegetable oil, for frying
- Shredded lettuce (optional, for garnish)
- Diced tomatoes (optional, for garnish)
- Sour cream (optional, for garnish)
- Salsa or guacamole (optional, for garnish)

Instructions:

1. **Prepare the Filling:**
   - In a large skillet over medium heat, cook the ground beef until browned, breaking it up with a spoon.
   - Drain any excess fat if needed.
   - Add the chopped onion and cook until softened, about 5 minutes.
   - Stir in the minced garlic and bell pepper (if using), and cook for another 2 minutes.
   - Add the taco seasoning mix and tomato sauce. Stir to combine.
   - If using, add the black beans and cooked rice, mixing everything well.
   - Season with salt and pepper to taste.
   - Stir in the shredded cheese until melted and combined with the filling. Remove from heat and set aside.
2. **Assemble the Chimichangas:**
   - Warm the tortillas in a dry skillet or microwave to make them more pliable.
   - Place a tortilla on a flat surface.
   - Spoon about 1/4 to 1/3 cup of the filling into the center of the tortilla.

- Fold in the sides of the tortilla and roll it up from the bottom, making sure the filling is fully enclosed and the ends are tucked in.
3. **Fry the Chimichangas:**
    - Heat about 2 inches of vegetable oil in a large, heavy-bottomed skillet or Dutch oven over medium-high heat.
    - Once the oil is hot (about 350°F or 175°C), carefully place the chimichangas seam-side down in the hot oil.
    - Fry until golden brown and crispy, about 3-4 minutes per side.
    - Use tongs to turn them carefully and ensure even browning.
    - Remove the chimichangas from the oil and drain on paper towels.
4. **Serve:**
    - Garnish with shredded lettuce, diced tomatoes, sour cream, and your favorite salsa or guacamole, if desired.

Enjoy your crispy, delicious Chimichangas!

Tamales

Ingredients:

For the Masa:

- 4 cups masa harina (corn flour for tamales)
- 1 cup lard or vegetable shortening
- 2 teaspoons baking powder
- 1 teaspoon salt
- 2 cups chicken or vegetable broth (more if needed)

For the Filling:

- 2 cups shredded pork (or chicken, beef, or cheese)
- 1 cup red chili sauce or salsa
- 1 cup cooked black beans (optional)
- 1/2 cup chopped green chilies (optional)
- 1/2 cup finely chopped onion (optional)
- 1/2 teaspoon cumin (optional)
- 1/2 teaspoon garlic powder (optional)

For Wrapping:

- 30-40 dried corn husks, soaked in warm water for at least 1 hour

Instructions:

1. **Prepare the Corn Husks:**
   - Soak the dried corn husks in a large bowl of warm water for at least 1 hour to soften them. Drain and pat dry.
2. **Prepare the Filling:**
   - In a bowl, combine the shredded meat with red chili sauce or salsa. If using, mix in black beans, green chilies, chopped onion, cumin, and garlic powder. Set aside.
3. **Prepare the Masa:**
   - In a large mixing bowl, combine masa harina, baking powder, and salt.
   - Add the lard or vegetable shortening and mix until the mixture resembles coarse crumbs.
   - Gradually add the chicken or vegetable broth, mixing until the masa becomes a soft, spreadable dough. The masa should be moist but not too wet.
4. **Assemble the Tamales:**
   - Take a soaked corn husk and spread a portion of the masa dough in the center, leaving a border on the sides and bottom.

- Place a spoonful of the filling on top of the masa.
- Fold the sides of the husk over the masa and filling, then fold up the bottom to seal the tamale.
- Repeat with the remaining husks, masa, and filling.
5. **Steam the Tamales:**
    - Arrange the tamales upright in a large steamer or a stockpot fitted with a steaming rack. If needed, place a small crumpled piece of foil or additional husks between the tamales to keep them upright.
    - Cover the tamales with a damp cloth or additional husks to keep them moist.
    - Steam over medium heat for about 1.5 to 2 hours, or until the masa is firm and separates easily from the husks. Check occasionally and add more water to the steamer as needed.
6. **Serve:**
    - Let the tamales cool slightly before serving. Serve with salsa, sour cream, or your favorite condiments.

Enjoy your homemade Tamales!

Quesadillas

Ingredients:

For the Quesadillas:

- 8 flour tortillas (8-inch or 10-inch)
- 2 cups shredded cheese (cheddar, Monterey Jack, or a blend)
- 1 cup cooked and shredded chicken, beef, or other filling (optional)
- 1 small onion, finely chopped (optional)
- 1 bell pepper, finely chopped (optional)
- 1/2 cup mushrooms, sliced (optional)
- 2 tablespoons vegetable oil or butter
- Salt and pepper, to taste

For Serving (optional):

- Salsa
- Guacamole
- Sour cream
- Fresh cilantro, chopped

Instructions:

1. **Prepare the Filling:**
    - If using additional fillings like cooked chicken, beef, onions, bell peppers, or mushrooms, sauté them in a skillet with a little oil until tender and cooked through. Season with salt and pepper to taste.
2. **Assemble the Quesadillas:**
    - Heat a large skillet or griddle over medium heat.
    - Place a tortilla in the skillet and sprinkle about 1/2 cup of shredded cheese evenly over half of the tortilla.
    - Add a portion of any additional filling (chicken, vegetables, etc.) on top of the cheese.
    - Fold the tortilla in half to cover the filling, pressing down gently with a spatula.
3. **Cook the Quesadillas:**
    - Cook for 2-3 minutes on one side, or until the tortilla is golden brown and the cheese is melted.
    - Flip the quesadilla carefully and cook for another 2-3 minutes on the other side until golden brown and crispy.
    - Remove from the skillet and let cool for a minute before cutting.
4. **Serve:**
    - Cut the quesadilla into wedges and serve with salsa, guacamole, sour cream, and chopped fresh cilantro if desired.

Enjoy your tasty and versatile Quesadillas!

Fish Tacos

Ingredients:

For the Fish:

- 1 lb white fish fillets (like cod, tilapia, or mahi-mahi)
- 1 cup all-purpose flour
- 1 teaspoon paprika
- 1/2 teaspoon garlic powder
- 1/2 teaspoon onion powder
- 1/2 teaspoon cayenne pepper (optional, for extra heat)
- 1/2 teaspoon salt
- 1/4 teaspoon black pepper
- 1 cup buttermilk (or regular milk)
- Vegetable oil, for frying

For the Slaw:

- 2 cups shredded cabbage (green or purple, or a mix)
- 1 cup shredded carrots
- 1/4 cup chopped fresh cilantro
- 2 tablespoons lime juice
- 1 tablespoon honey or sugar
- Salt and pepper, to taste

For the Sauce:

- 1/2 cup sour cream or Greek yogurt
- 1/4 cup mayonnaise
- 1 tablespoon lime juice
- 1 tablespoon chopped fresh cilantro
- 1 teaspoon honey or sugar
- 1/2 teaspoon garlic powder
- Salt and pepper, to taste

For Assembly:

- 8 small corn or flour tortillas
- Lime wedges
- Fresh cilantro, chopped (optional, for garnish)

Instructions:

1. **Prepare the Slaw:**
   - In a large bowl, combine shredded cabbage, shredded carrots, and chopped cilantro.
   - In a small bowl, whisk together lime juice, honey or sugar, salt, and pepper.
   - Pour the dressing over the cabbage mixture and toss to coat. Set aside.
2. **Prepare the Sauce:**
   - In a small bowl, mix together sour cream or Greek yogurt, mayonnaise, lime juice, chopped cilantro, honey or sugar, garlic powder, salt, and pepper. Adjust seasoning to taste. Set aside.
3. **Prepare the Fish:**
   - In a shallow bowl, mix flour, paprika, garlic powder, onion powder, cayenne pepper, salt, and black pepper.
   - Dip each fish fillet into the buttermilk, allowing any excess to drip off, then dredge in the seasoned flour mixture, coating evenly.
   - Heat vegetable oil in a large skillet over medium-high heat. The oil should be about 1/4 inch deep.
   - Fry the fish fillets in batches, for 3-4 minutes per side, or until golden brown and crispy. Drain on paper towels.
4. **Assemble the Tacos:**
   - Warm the tortillas in a dry skillet or microwave until pliable.
   - Slice the cooked fish into bite-sized pieces.
   - Place a few pieces of fish on each tortilla.
   - Top with a generous portion of slaw and a drizzle of the sauce.
   - Garnish with additional cilantro and lime wedges if desired.
5. **Serve:**
   - Serve the fish tacos immediately, with extra lime wedges and cilantro on the side.

Enjoy your delicious and fresh Fish Tacos!

Huevos Rancheros

Ingredients:

For the Ranchero Sauce:

- 2 tablespoons vegetable oil
- 1 small onion, finely chopped
- 2 cloves garlic, minced
- 1 can (14.5 oz) diced tomatoes (or 2 cups fresh tomatoes, chopped)
- 1-2 jalapeño peppers, seeded and minced (adjust to heat preference)
- 1 teaspoon ground cumin
- 1 teaspoon chili powder
- 1/2 teaspoon dried oregano
- Salt and pepper, to taste

For the Huevos Rancheros:

- 4 large eggs
- 4 corn tortillas
- 1 cup black beans, cooked and drained (optional)
- 1/2 cup crumbled queso fresco or shredded cheddar cheese (optional)
- Fresh cilantro, chopped (optional, for garnish)
- Lime wedges (optional, for serving)

Instructions:

1. **Prepare the Ranchero Sauce:**
    - Heat vegetable oil in a medium saucepan over medium heat.
    - Add the chopped onion and cook until softened, about 5 minutes.
    - Stir in the minced garlic and cook for another minute.
    - Add the diced tomatoes (with their juice), minced jalapeños, ground cumin, chili powder, and dried oregano.
    - Bring to a simmer, then reduce heat and cook for about 10-15 minutes, until the sauce thickens slightly.
    - Season with salt and pepper to taste. Keep warm.
2. **Prepare the Tortillas:**
    - In a large skillet, heat a little vegetable oil over medium heat.
    - Warm the corn tortillas in the skillet for about 30 seconds per side, until soft and pliable. Keep warm.
3. **Cook the Eggs:**
    - In a separate non-stick skillet, heat a small amount of oil over medium heat.

- Crack the eggs into the skillet and cook to your desired doneness. For traditional Huevos Rancheros, the eggs are usually cooked sunny-side up or over-easy. Season with a pinch of salt and pepper.

4. **Assemble the Dish:**
   - Place a warm tortilla on each plate.
   - Spread a layer of cooked black beans (if using) on each tortilla.
   - Top with a fried egg.
   - Spoon the warm ranchero sauce over the egg.
   - Sprinkle with crumbled queso fresco or shredded cheddar cheese if desired.

5. **Garnish and Serve:**
   - Garnish with chopped fresh cilantro and serve with lime wedges on the side.

Enjoy your classic Huevos Rancheros, a satisfying and flavorful start to your day!

Mexican Street Corn (Elote)

Ingredients:

- 4 ears of corn, husked and cleaned
- 1/2 cup mayonnaise
- 1/2 cup sour cream
- 1 cup cotija cheese, crumbled (or feta cheese as a substitute)
- 2-3 tablespoons chili powder (adjust to taste)
- 1 tablespoon lime juice (plus extra lime wedges for serving)
- 2 cloves garlic, minced
- 1/4 teaspoon ground cumin
- Salt, to taste
- Fresh cilantro, chopped (optional, for garnish)

Instructions:

1. **Prepare the Corn:**
   - Preheat your grill to medium-high heat.
   - Place the cleaned ears of corn on the grill. Grill for about 10-15 minutes, turning occasionally, until the corn is charred and cooked through.
2. **Prepare the Sauce:**
   - In a medium bowl, combine mayonnaise, sour cream, minced garlic, lime juice, ground cumin, and salt. Mix well.
   - Stir in the crumbled cotija cheese, reserving a small amount for sprinkling on top later.
3. **Coat the Corn:**
   - Once the corn is grilled and charred to your liking, remove it from the grill.
   - While the corn is still hot, brush or spread the prepared sauce evenly over each ear of corn.
   - Sprinkle additional cotija cheese over the top, and dust with chili powder to taste.
4. **Garnish and Serve:**
   - Garnish with freshly chopped cilantro if desired.
   - Serve with lime wedges on the side for an extra squeeze of tangy lime juice.

Enjoy your delicious Mexican Street Corn (Elote)!

Pozole

Ingredients:

For the Stew:

- 2 lbs pork shoulder or pork loin, cut into bite-sized pieces
- 2 tablespoons vegetable oil
- 1 large onion, chopped
- 4 cloves garlic, minced
- 2-3 dried ancho chilies, stemmed and seeded (or use 2 tablespoons ancho chili powder)
- 1-2 dried pasilla chilies, stemmed and seeded (optional, or use 1 tablespoon pasilla chili powder)
- 1 teaspoon dried oregano
- 1 teaspoon ground cumin
- 1 can (15 oz) hominy, drained and rinsed
- 6 cups chicken or pork broth
- Salt and pepper, to taste
- 2 bay leaves

For Garnishing:

- 1 small cabbage, shredded
- 1 radish, thinly sliced
- 1-2 limes, cut into wedges
- 1/2 cup chopped fresh cilantro
- 1/2 cup diced onion
- Sliced jalapeños (optional)
- Tortilla chips or tostadas

Instructions:

1. **Prepare the Chilies:**
    - If using dried chilies, toast them lightly in a dry skillet over medium heat until fragrant, about 1-2 minutes. Be careful not to burn them.
    - Transfer the toasted chilies to a bowl and cover with hot water. Let them soak for about 15 minutes until softened.
    - Drain the chilies and blend them with a little water in a blender or food processor until smooth. If using chili powder, skip this step.
2. **Cook the Pork:**
    - Heat vegetable oil in a large pot or Dutch oven over medium-high heat.
    - Add the chopped onion and cook until softened, about 5 minutes.
    - Stir in the minced garlic and cook for another minute.
    - Add the pork pieces and cook until browned on all sides.

- Stir in the blended chilies (or chili powder), oregano, and cumin. Cook for 1-2 minutes until fragrant.
3. **Simmer the Stew:**
    - Add the hominy, broth, and bay leaves to the pot. Stir to combine.
    - Bring to a boil, then reduce heat to low and simmer for about 1.5 to 2 hours, or until the pork is tender and the flavors have melded together.
    - Season with salt and pepper to taste.
4. **Serve:**
    - Remove the bay leaves from the stew.
    - Ladle the pozole into bowls and serve with garnishes on the side.
    - Let everyone add shredded cabbage, radish slices, lime wedges, chopped cilantro, diced onion, and sliced jalapeños to their liking.
    - Serve with tortilla chips or tostadas.

Enjoy your hearty and flavorful Pozole!

Chicken Mole

Ingredients:

For the Mole Sauce:

- 2 tablespoons vegetable oil
- 1 large onion, finely chopped
- 4 cloves garlic, minced
- 2 dried ancho chilies, stemmed and seeded
- 2 dried pasilla chilies, stemmed and seeded (optional)
- 2 tablespoons sesame seeds
- 1/4 cup almonds, chopped
- 1/4 cup raisins
- 1/4 cup unsweetened cocoa powder
- 1/2 cup tomato paste
- 1/2 teaspoon ground cumin
- 1/2 teaspoon dried oregano
- 2 cups chicken broth
- 2 tablespoons brown sugar
- Salt and pepper, to taste

For the Chicken:

- 4 bone-in, skinless chicken thighs
- 4 bone-in, skinless chicken drumsticks
- Salt and pepper, to taste

Instructions:

1. **Prepare the Mole Sauce:**
    - Heat vegetable oil in a large skillet or saucepan over medium heat.
    - Add the chopped onion and cook until softened, about 5 minutes.
    - Stir in the minced garlic and cook for another minute.
    - Toast the dried chilies in a dry skillet over medium heat until fragrant, about 1-2 minutes. Be careful not to burn them.
    - Transfer the toasted chilies to a bowl, cover with hot water, and let them soak for about 15 minutes until softened. Drain.
    - Blend the softened chilies with a little of the soaking water in a blender or food processor until smooth.
    - In the same skillet with the onions and garlic, add sesame seeds, chopped almonds, and raisins. Cook for 2-3 minutes, stirring frequently, until fragrant and lightly toasted.

- Stir in cocoa powder, tomato paste, cumin, and oregano. Cook for another 2 minutes.
- Add the blended chilies and chicken broth. Bring to a simmer and cook for about 15 minutes, stirring occasionally, until the sauce thickens slightly.
- Stir in the brown sugar and season with salt and pepper to taste. Adjust seasoning as needed. Set aside.

2. **Prepare the Chicken:**
    - Season the chicken thighs and drumsticks with salt and pepper.
    - In a large skillet or Dutch oven, heat a little vegetable oil over medium-high heat.
    - Brown the chicken pieces on all sides until golden brown, about 5-7 minutes per side. The chicken does not need to be fully cooked at this stage.

3. **Combine Chicken and Mole Sauce:**
    - Pour the prepared mole sauce over the browned chicken in the skillet or Dutch oven.
    - Bring to a simmer, cover, and cook for 30-40 minutes, or until the chicken is cooked through and tender.
    - Occasionally check the chicken and sauce, and add a bit more chicken broth if the sauce gets too thick.

4. **Serve:**
    - Serve the Chicken Mole hot with rice, warm tortillas, or Mexican-style sides.
    - Garnish with chopped fresh cilantro if desired.

Enjoy your rich and flavorful Chicken Mole!

Chiles Rellenos

Ingredients:

For the Chiles:

- 6-8 large poblano peppers
- 1 cup shredded cheese (such as Oaxaca, Monterrey Jack, or a blend)
- 1/2 cup cooked ground beef or pork (optional)
- 1/2 cup cooked rice (optional)
- Salt and pepper, to taste

For the Batter:

- 4 large eggs
- 1/2 cup all-purpose flour
- 1/2 teaspoon baking powder
- 1/4 teaspoon salt

For Frying:

- Vegetable oil

For Serving (optional):

- Tomato sauce or salsa
- Fresh cilantro, chopped

Instructions:

1. **Prepare the Peppers:**
   - Preheat your oven to 400°F (200°C).
   - Place the poblano peppers on a baking sheet and roast them in the oven for 20-25 minutes, turning occasionally, until the skin is blistered and charred.
   - Remove the peppers from the oven and place them in a bowl. Cover the bowl with plastic wrap and let them steam for about 10 minutes. This makes peeling easier.
   - Carefully peel off the charred skin from each pepper. Make a small slit along one side of each pepper and remove the seeds and membranes. Be careful not to tear the peppers.
2. **Prepare the Filling:**
   - In a bowl, mix the shredded cheese with cooked ground beef or pork (if using) and cooked rice (if using). Season with salt and pepper.
3. **Stuff the Peppers:**

- Gently stuff each pepper with the cheese mixture. If the filling is too loose, you can use toothpicks to secure the open edges of the peppers.

4. **Prepare the Batter:**
    - In a large bowl, separate the egg whites from the yolks.
    - Beat the egg whites with an electric mixer until stiff peaks form.
    - In another bowl, whisk the egg yolks with flour, baking powder, and salt until smooth.
    - Gently fold the egg yolk mixture into the beaten egg whites until just combined.

5. **Fry the Peppers:**
    - Heat about 1-2 inches of vegetable oil in a large skillet over medium-high heat.
    - Dip each stuffed pepper into the batter, coating it evenly.
    - Carefully place the battered peppers into the hot oil. Fry in batches, turning occasionally, until golden brown and crispy, about 3-4 minutes per side.
    - Use tongs to remove the peppers from the oil and drain them on paper towels.

6. **Serve:**
    - Serve the Chiles Rellenos hot with tomato sauce or salsa, and garnish with fresh cilantro if desired.

Enjoy your delicious and savory Chiles Rellenos!

Sopes

Ingredients:

For the Sopes:

- 2 cups masa harina (corn flour for tortillas)
- 1 1/4 cups warm water
- 1/2 teaspoon salt
- Vegetable oil (for cooking)

For the Toppings:

- 1 cup refried beans (black or pinto beans)
- 1 cup cooked and seasoned ground beef, shredded chicken, or pork (optional)
- 1 cup shredded lettuce
- 1/2 cup diced tomatoes
- 1/4 cup finely chopped onions
- 1/4 cup sour cream or Mexican crema
- 1/2 cup crumbled queso fresco or shredded cheese
- Salsa or hot sauce (optional)
- Fresh cilantro, chopped (optional)
- Lime wedges (optional)

Instructions:

1. **Prepare the Masa:**
   - In a large bowl, combine the masa harina and salt.
   - Gradually add warm water, mixing until a smooth, pliable dough forms. The dough should be moist but not sticky. Adjust with more water or masa harina if needed.
2. **Shape the Sopes:**
   - Divide the dough into 8-10 equal portions and roll each portion into a ball.
   - Flatten each ball between two pieces of plastic wrap or parchment paper using a tortilla press or a rolling pin, to form a small, thick tortilla (about 1/4 inch thick).
   - Using your fingers, pinch the edges of each tortilla to create a raised border around the edge, forming a small rim to hold the toppings.
3. **Cook the Sopes:**
   - Heat a dry skillet or griddle over medium-high heat.
   - Cook each sope for about 1-2 minutes per side, until lightly browned and cooked through.
   - Remove from the skillet and set aside. If needed, gently press the edges to maintain their shape.
4. **Assemble the Sopes:**

- Heat a small amount of vegetable oil in a skillet over medium heat.
- Spread a layer of refried beans over each sope.
- Top with your choice of cooked meat, if using.
- Add shredded lettuce, diced tomatoes, and chopped onions.
- Drizzle with sour cream or Mexican crema and sprinkle with crumbled queso fresco or shredded cheese.
- Garnish with fresh cilantro and serve with salsa or hot sauce on the side.

5. **Serve:**
   - Serve the sopes immediately, with lime wedges on the side for added freshness.

Enjoy your delicious and customizable Sopes!

Flautas

Ingredients:

For the Filling:

- 2 cups cooked, shredded chicken, beef, or pork
- 1 small onion, finely chopped
- 2 cloves garlic, minced
- 1 teaspoon ground cumin
- 1 teaspoon chili powder
- 1/2 teaspoon paprika
- 1/2 teaspoon dried oregano
- 1/2 cup chicken or beef broth
- Salt and pepper, to taste

For the Flautas:

- 12-15 small flour or corn tortillas (small size works best for flautas)
- Vegetable oil, for frying

For Serving (optional):

- Shredded lettuce
- Diced tomatoes
- Sliced avocado or guacamole
- Sour cream
- Salsa
- Fresh cilantro, chopped
- Lime wedges

Instructions:

1. **Prepare the Filling:**
    - In a large skillet over medium heat, add a small amount of oil and cook the chopped onion until softened, about 5 minutes.
    - Add the minced garlic and cook for another minute.
    - Stir in the shredded meat, ground cumin, chili powder, paprika, and dried oregano. Mix well.
    - Add the broth and cook, stirring occasionally, until the mixture is heated through and any liquid has evaporated. Season with salt and pepper to taste.
    - Remove from heat and let cool slightly.
2. **Prepare the Tortillas:**

- If using corn tortillas, warm them slightly in a dry skillet or microwave to make them more pliable. This helps prevent cracking when rolling.
3. **Assemble the Flautas:**
    - Place a small amount of the filling along one edge of each tortilla.
    - Roll the tortilla tightly around the filling, securing it with a toothpick if needed.
4. **Fry the Flautas:**
    - Heat about 2 inches of vegetable oil in a large skillet or Dutch oven over medium-high heat.
    - Once the oil is hot (about 350°F or 175°C), carefully place a few flautas in the hot oil, being careful not to overcrowd the pan.
    - Fry the flautas, turning occasionally, until golden brown and crispy, about 2-3 minutes per side.
    - Use tongs to remove the flautas from the oil and drain on paper towels.
5. **Serve:**
    - Remove toothpicks if used.
    - Serve the flautas hot with your choice of toppings like shredded lettuce, diced tomatoes, sliced avocado or guacamole, sour cream, salsa, and fresh cilantro.
    - Add lime wedges on the side for extra tang.

Enjoy your crispy and delicious Flautas!

Mexican Rice

Ingredients:

- 2 tablespoons vegetable oil
- 1 cup long-grain white rice
- 1 small onion, finely chopped
- 2 cloves garlic, minced
- 1/2 cup tomato sauce or crushed tomatoes
- 2 cups chicken or vegetable broth
- 1/2 teaspoon ground cumin
- 1/2 teaspoon chili powder
- 1/2 teaspoon paprika
- Salt, to taste
- 1/4 cup frozen peas or diced carrots (optional)
- 1/4 cup chopped fresh cilantro (optional, for garnish)
- Lime wedges (optional, for serving)

Instructions:

1. **Prepare the Rice:**
   - Heat the vegetable oil in a large skillet or saucepan over medium heat.
   - Add the rice and cook, stirring frequently, until the rice is lightly toasted and golden brown, about 3-4 minutes.
2. **Cook the Aromatics:**
   - Add the chopped onion to the skillet with the rice and cook until softened, about 5 minutes.
   - Stir in the minced garlic and cook for another minute.
3. **Add Tomato and Spices:**
   - Stir in the tomato sauce or crushed tomatoes, ground cumin, chili powder, paprika, and salt. Cook for about 2 minutes, allowing the flavors to meld.
4. **Simmer the Rice:**
   - Pour in the chicken or vegetable broth and bring to a boil.
   - Reduce the heat to low, cover the skillet or saucepan with a lid, and simmer for about 20 minutes, or until the rice is tender and the liquid is absorbed. Do not stir the rice while it's cooking, as this can make it sticky.
5. **Add Vegetables (Optional):**
   - If using, stir in the frozen peas or diced carrots during the last 5 minutes of cooking.
6. **Finish and Serve:**
   - Remove the skillet or saucepan from heat and let it sit, covered, for an additional 5 minutes.
   - Fluff the rice with a fork and stir in chopped fresh cilantro if desired.

- Serve with lime wedges on the side for added freshness.

Enjoy your flavorful Mexican Rice with your favorite Mexican dishes!

Refried Beans

Ingredients:

- 2 cups dried pinto beans
- 6 cups water (for soaking and cooking)
- 1 small onion, chopped
- 2 cloves garlic, minced
- 1-2 tablespoons vegetable oil or lard
- 1 teaspoon ground cumin
- 1/2 teaspoon chili powder (optional)
- Salt, to taste
- Freshly ground black pepper, to taste

Instructions:

1. **Prepare the Beans:**
    - Rinse the dried pinto beans under cold water.
    - In a large bowl, cover the beans with water and let them soak overnight, or at least 8 hours. This helps to soften the beans and reduce cooking time.
2. **Cook the Beans:**
    - Drain and rinse the soaked beans.
    - In a large pot, add the beans and 6 cups of fresh water.
    - Bring to a boil over medium-high heat. Reduce heat to low and simmer, partially covered, for about 1.5 to 2 hours, or until the beans are tender.
    - Check occasionally and add more water if necessary to keep the beans covered.
3. **Prepare the Refried Beans:**
    - In a large skillet or frying pan, heat the vegetable oil or lard over medium heat.
    - Add the chopped onion and cook until softened and translucent, about 5 minutes.
    - Stir in the minced garlic and cook for another minute.
    - Using a slotted spoon, transfer the cooked beans from the pot to the skillet, leaving some of the bean cooking liquid behind.
    - Add ground cumin and chili powder (if using). Mash the beans with a potato masher or the back of a spoon until you reach your desired consistency. You can also use an immersion blender for a smoother texture.
    - Gradually add some of the reserved bean cooking liquid to achieve your preferred consistency. The beans should be creamy but not too runny.
    - Season with salt and freshly ground black pepper to taste.
4. **Simmer:**
    - Continue to cook the beans over medium heat, stirring frequently, for another 5-10 minutes, allowing the flavors to meld and the beans to thicken.
5. **Serve:**

- Serve the refried beans hot as a side dish or as a filling for tacos, burritos, or enchiladas.

Enjoy your homemade Refried Beans!

Guacamole

Ingredients:

- 3 ripe avocados
- 1 small onion, finely chopped
- 2 cloves garlic, minced
- 1-2 medium tomatoes, diced (seeds removed)
- 1 jalapeño pepper, seeded and finely chopped (optional, for heat)
- 1/4 cup fresh cilantro, chopped
- 1 lime, juiced (or more to taste)
- Salt, to taste
- Freshly ground black pepper, to taste

Instructions:

1. **Prepare the Avocados:**
     - Cut the avocados in half and remove the pits. Scoop the flesh into a large mixing bowl.
     - Use a fork to mash the avocados to your desired consistency—smooth or slightly chunky.
2. **Add the Vegetables:**
     - Stir in the finely chopped onion, minced garlic, diced tomatoes, and jalapeño pepper (if using).
3. **Season the Guacamole:**
     - Add the chopped cilantro and lime juice to the bowl.
     - Season with salt and freshly ground black pepper to taste. Mix well.
4. **Adjust and Serve:**
     - Taste the guacamole and adjust seasoning or lime juice as needed.
     - For best results, serve immediately with tortilla chips, tacos, or as a topping for your favorite Mexican dishes.

Note: If you need to store guacamole, place it in an airtight container and press a piece of plastic wrap directly onto the surface of the guacamole to minimize browning. It's best enjoyed fresh, but it can be refrigerated for up to a day.

Enjoy your fresh and creamy Guacamole!

Salsa Verde

Ingredients:

- 1 lb (450g) tomatillos, husked and rinsed
- 1-2 jalapeño peppers or serrano peppers (adjust to taste), stemmed and seeded
- 1 small onion, chopped
- 2 cloves garlic, minced
- 1/2 cup fresh cilantro, chopped
- 1 tablespoon lime juice (about 1 lime)
- Salt, to taste
- Freshly ground black pepper, to taste

Instructions:

1. **Roast the Tomatillos and Peppers:**
   - Preheat your oven to 400°F (200°C).
   - Place the tomatillos and peppers on a baking sheet. Roast in the oven for about 10-15 minutes, or until the tomatillos are soft and slightly charred. You can also roast them under the broiler, turning occasionally, until they're nicely charred.
2. **Blend the Salsa:**
   - Transfer the roasted tomatillos and peppers to a blender or food processor. Add the chopped onion, minced garlic, and cilantro.
   - Blend until smooth. If the salsa is too thick, you can add a little water to reach your desired consistency.
3. **Season the Salsa:**
   - Stir in the lime juice.
   - Season with salt and freshly ground black pepper to taste. Adjust the seasoning as needed.
4. **Serve:**
   - Serve the Salsa Verde immediately with tortilla chips, or as a topping for tacos, grilled meats, or any dish that could use a zesty kick.
   - Salsa Verde can be stored in an airtight container in the refrigerator for up to a week.

Enjoy your vibrant and flavorful Salsa Verde!

Pico de Gallo

Ingredients:

- 4 ripe tomatoes, diced
- 1 small onion, finely chopped
- 1-2 jalapeño peppers, seeded and finely chopped (adjust to taste)
- 1/2 cup fresh cilantro, chopped
- 1 lime, juiced
- Salt, to taste
- Freshly ground black pepper, to taste

Instructions:

1. **Prepare the Ingredients:**
    - Dice the tomatoes and place them in a large mixing bowl.
    - Finely chop the onion and add it to the bowl.
    - Seed and finely chop the jalapeño peppers (wear gloves if you have sensitive skin) and add them to the bowl.
    - Chop the fresh cilantro and add it to the bowl.
2. **Mix and Season:**
    - Squeeze the juice of the lime over the mixture.
    - Season with salt and freshly ground black pepper to taste.
    - Gently stir everything together until well combined.
3. **Adjust and Serve:**
    - Taste the Pico de Gallo and adjust the seasoning or lime juice as needed.
    - Let it sit for about 15 minutes to allow the flavors to meld together.
    - Serve with tortilla chips or as a fresh topping for tacos, grilled meats, or any dish of your choice.

Tip: Pico de Gallo is best enjoyed fresh, but it can be stored in an airtight container in the refrigerator for up to 2 days. If you find that the tomatoes release too much liquid, you can drain some off before serving.

Enjoy your crisp and flavorful Pico de Gallo!

Ceviche

Ingredients:

For the Ceviche:

- 1 lb (450g) fresh firm white fish (such as tilapia, sea bass, or cod), cut into small cubes or 1 lb (450g) raw shrimp, peeled, deveined, and chopped
- 1 cup fresh lime juice (about 6-8 limes)
- 1/2 cup fresh lemon juice (about 2 lemons)
- 1 small red onion, finely chopped
- 1-2 serrano or jalapeño peppers, seeded and finely chopped (adjust to taste)
- 1 cup diced tomatoes (seeds removed)
- 1/2 cup chopped fresh cilantro
- 1 cucumber, peeled, seeded, and diced (optional)
- 1 avocado, diced (optional)
- Salt, to taste
- Freshly ground black pepper, to taste

For Serving:

- Tortilla chips or tostadas
- Lime wedges

Instructions:

1. **Marinate the Seafood:**
   - In a large glass or ceramic bowl, combine the fish or shrimp with lime juice and lemon juice. Make sure the seafood is fully submerged in the juice.
   - Cover the bowl and refrigerate for 2-4 hours, or until the seafood is opaque and "cooked" by the citrus juice. For shrimp, this usually takes about 2 hours.
2. **Prepare the Vegetables:**
   - While the seafood is marinating, prepare the red onion, serrano or jalapeño peppers, tomatoes, cilantro, and cucumber (if using).
3. **Combine Ingredients:**
   - Once the seafood is "cooked," drain some of the citrus juice if there's too much liquid left.
   - Add the prepared vegetables, chopped cilantro, and diced avocado (if using) to the bowl with the seafood. Gently toss to combine.
   - Season with salt and freshly ground black pepper to taste. Adjust seasoning as needed.
4. **Serve:**
   - Serve the ceviche chilled with tortilla chips, tostadas, or on its own as a light and refreshing dish.

    - Garnish with additional cilantro and lime wedges if desired.

Note: Ceviche should be consumed within a day or two of preparation for the best flavor and texture. If storing leftovers, keep them in an airtight container in the refrigerator.

Enjoy your vibrant and delicious Ceviche!

Tostadas

Ingredients:

For the Tostada Shells:

- 8-10 corn tortillas
- Vegetable oil (for frying)

For the Toppings (suggested):

- Refried beans (recipe above)
- Shredded lettuce
- Diced tomatoes
- Chopped onions
- Sliced avocado or guacamole
- Shredded cheese (such as queso fresco, Monterey Jack, or Cheddar)
- Salsa or Pico de Gallo (recipes above)
- Sour cream
- Fresh cilantro, chopped
- Lime wedges

Instructions:

1. **Prepare the Tostada Shells:**
    - Heat about 1/2 inch of vegetable oil in a large skillet over medium-high heat.
    - Carefully place a tortilla in the hot oil, using tongs to hold it down and shape it into a flat, round shell. Fry for about 1-2 minutes on each side, or until golden brown and crispy.
    - Remove the tostada shell from the oil and drain on paper towels. Repeat with the remaining tortillas. You can also bake the tortillas for a healthier option:
        - Preheat the oven to 400°F (200°C).
        - Place the tortillas on a baking sheet in a single layer.
        - Bake for about 5-7 minutes on each side, or until crisp and golden.
2. **Assemble the Tostadas:**
    - Spread a layer of refried beans on each tostada shell.
    - Add your choice of toppings, such as shredded lettuce, diced tomatoes, chopped onions, sliced avocado or guacamole, and shredded cheese.
    - Drizzle with salsa or Pico de Gallo, and top with a dollop of sour cream.
    - Garnish with chopped fresh cilantro.
3. **Serve:**
    - Serve the tostadas immediately, as they are best enjoyed crispy and fresh.
    - Provide lime wedges on the side for added flavor.

Tip: You can customize the toppings based on your preferences, such as adding seasoned ground beef, shredded chicken, or other favorite ingredients.

Enjoy your crispy and flavorful Tostadas!

Albondigas (Mexican Meatballs)

Ingredients:

For the Meatballs:

- 1 lb (450g) ground beef (or a mix of beef and pork)
- 1/2 cup cooked rice (white or brown)
- 1/4 cup finely chopped onion
- 2 cloves garlic, minced
- 1/4 cup fresh cilantro, chopped
- 1 egg
- 1/2 teaspoon ground cumin
- 1/2 teaspoon dried oregano
- 1/2 teaspoon paprika
- Salt, to taste
- Freshly ground black pepper, to taste

For the Soup/Base:

- 1 tablespoon vegetable oil
- 1 small onion, chopped
- 2 cloves garlic, minced
- 1 cup tomato sauce or crushed tomatoes
- 4 cups beef or chicken broth
- 1-2 carrots, peeled and sliced
- 2-3 potatoes, peeled and cubed
- 1 zucchini, sliced
- 1/2 cup frozen peas (optional)
- 1 bay leaf
- 1 teaspoon dried oregano
- Salt, to taste
- Freshly ground black pepper, to taste

Instructions:

1. **Prepare the Meatballs:**
    - In a large bowl, combine the ground beef, cooked rice, chopped onion, minced garlic, cilantro, egg, ground cumin, dried oregano, paprika, salt, and pepper.
    - Mix until well combined, but avoid overmixing to keep the meatballs tender.
    - Shape the mixture into 1-1.5 inch meatballs and set aside.
2. **Prepare the Soup/Base:**
    - Heat the vegetable oil in a large pot over medium heat.
    - Add the chopped onion and cook until softened, about 5 minutes.

- Stir in the minced garlic and cook for another minute.
- Add the tomato sauce or crushed tomatoes and cook for 2-3 minutes, stirring occasionally.

3. **Cook the Albondigas:**
   - Pour in the beef or chicken broth and bring to a boil.
   - Gently add the meatballs to the pot, one by one, being careful not to overcrowd.
   - Reduce the heat to a simmer and add the sliced carrots, cubed potatoes, and bay leaf.
   - Cover and simmer for about 20-25 minutes, or until the meatballs are cooked through and the vegetables are tender.

4. **Finish the Soup:**
   - Add the sliced zucchini and frozen peas (if using) and cook for another 5-10 minutes, until the zucchini is tender.
   - Season with dried oregano, salt, and freshly ground black pepper to taste.

5. **Serve:**
   - Serve the Albondigas hot in bowls with the broth and vegetables.
   - Garnish with additional chopped cilantro if desired.

Enjoy your hearty and flavorful Albondigas!

Queso Fundido

Ingredients:

- 2 cups shredded cheese (Mexican blend, Oaxaca cheese, or Monterey Jack work well)
- 1/2 cup crumbled chorizo (optional, for added flavor)
- 1/2 small onion, finely chopped
- 1-2 cloves garlic, minced
- 1/2 cup canned diced tomatoes (with or without green chilies, depending on your preference)
- 1/4 cup fresh cilantro, chopped (optional, for garnish)
- 1 tablespoon vegetable oil
- Salt, to taste
- Freshly ground black pepper, to taste

For Serving:

- Tortilla chips or sliced tortillas
- Fresh tortillas (for dipping)
- Pickled jalapeños or fresh salsa (optional, for extra flavor)

Instructions:

1. **Cook the Chorizo (if using):**
    - In a skillet over medium heat, cook the crumbled chorizo until browned and cooked through, about 5-7 minutes.
    - Remove the chorizo from the skillet and set aside. Drain excess fat if necessary.
2. **Prepare the Queso Fundido:**
    - In the same skillet (or a separate oven-safe dish), heat the vegetable oil over medium heat.
    - Add the chopped onion and cook until softened and translucent, about 5 minutes.
    - Stir in the minced garlic and cook for another minute.
    - Add the diced tomatoes and cook for an additional 2 minutes, allowing the flavors to meld.
3. **Add the Cheese:**
    - Reduce the heat to low. Add the shredded cheese to the skillet, stirring continuously until the cheese is fully melted and smooth.
    - If using chorizo, stir it back into the cheese mixture.
4. **Season and Garnish:**
    - Season with salt and freshly ground black pepper to taste.
    - Garnish with chopped fresh cilantro if desired.
5. **Serve:**
    - Serve the Queso Fundido hot, directly from the skillet or oven-safe dish.

- Provide tortilla chips or sliced tortillas for dipping. Fresh tortillas can also be warmed and used for dipping.
- Optional: Top with pickled jalapeños or fresh salsa for added flavor and heat.

Tip: For an extra touch, you can place the skillet under the broiler for a few minutes to get a crispy, golden top layer of cheese.

Enjoy your delicious and indulgent Queso Fundido!

Tamale Pie

Ingredients:

For the Meat Filling:

- 1 lb (450g) ground beef (or ground turkey)
- 1 small onion, chopped
- 2 cloves garlic, minced
- 1 cup corn kernels (fresh, frozen, or canned)
- 1 cup canned diced tomatoes
- 1/2 cup tomato sauce
- 1 tablespoon chili powder
- 1 teaspoon ground cumin
- 1/2 teaspoon paprika
- Salt, to taste
- Freshly ground black pepper, to taste
- 1 cup shredded cheese (cheddar, Monterey Jack, or a Mexican blend)

For the Cornbread Topping:

- 1 cup cornmeal
- 1 cup all-purpose flour
- 1/4 cup granulated sugar
- 1 tablespoon baking powder
- 1/2 teaspoon salt
- 1 cup milk
- 1/4 cup vegetable oil
- 1 large egg

Instructions:

1. **Prepare the Meat Filling:**
    - Preheat your oven to 375°F (190°C).
    - In a large skillet over medium heat, cook the ground beef until browned. Drain any excess fat.
    - Add the chopped onion and cook until softened, about 5 minutes.
    - Stir in the minced garlic and cook for another minute.
    - Add the corn kernels, diced tomatoes, tomato sauce, chili powder, ground cumin, paprika, salt, and pepper. Mix well.
    - Simmer for 10 minutes, stirring occasionally, until the mixture is heated through and slightly thickened.
2. **Prepare the Cornbread Topping:**
    - In a large bowl, combine the cornmeal, flour, sugar, baking powder, and salt.

- In a separate bowl, whisk together the milk, vegetable oil, and egg.
- Add the wet ingredients to the dry ingredients and mix until just combined. The batter will be thick.

3. **Assemble the Tamale Pie:**
   - Spread the meat filling evenly in a 9x13-inch baking dish or a similar oven-safe dish.
   - Sprinkle the shredded cheese evenly over the meat filling.
   - Spoon the cornbread batter over the top of the meat and cheese layer, spreading it out evenly with a spatula.
4. **Bake:**
   - Bake in the preheated oven for 25-30 minutes, or until the cornbread topping is golden brown and a toothpick inserted into the center comes out clean.
5. **Serve:**
   - Let the Tamale Pie cool slightly before serving.
   - Garnish with fresh cilantro, sour cream, or additional shredded cheese if desired.

Enjoy your hearty and satisfying Tamale Pie!

Enchilada Sauce

Ingredients:

- 2 tablespoons vegetable oil
- 1/4 cup chili powder
- 2 tablespoons all-purpose flour
- 1 cup tomato sauce
- 1 cup chicken or vegetable broth
- 1 tablespoon ground cumin
- 1 teaspoon garlic powder
- 1 teaspoon onion powder
- 1/2 teaspoon paprika
- 1/4 teaspoon cayenne pepper (optional, for extra heat)
- Salt, to taste
- Freshly ground black pepper, to taste

Instructions:

1. **Make the Roux:**
   - In a medium saucepan, heat the vegetable oil over medium heat.
   - Add the flour and cook, stirring constantly, for about 1-2 minutes until the flour is lightly toasted and forms a paste.
2. **Add the Chili Powder:**
   - Stir in the chili powder and cook for another 1-2 minutes, allowing the spices to bloom and become fragrant.
3. **Add Liquids and Spices:**
   - Gradually whisk in the tomato sauce and chicken or vegetable broth, making sure to smooth out any lumps.
   - Stir in the ground cumin, garlic powder, onion powder, paprika, and cayenne pepper (if using).
4. **Simmer the Sauce:**
   - Bring the mixture to a simmer, then reduce the heat to low.
   - Simmer for about 10-15 minutes, stirring occasionally, until the sauce has thickened to your desired consistency.
5. **Season and Adjust:**
   - Season the sauce with salt and freshly ground black pepper to taste.
   - Adjust any spices or heat level as desired.
6. **Serve or Store:**
   - Use the sauce immediately to smother enchiladas or as a base for other recipes.
   - Allow the sauce to cool before transferring it to an airtight container. It can be stored in the refrigerator for up to a week or frozen for up to 3 months.

Enjoy your flavorful homemade Enchilada Sauce!

Mexican Street Tacos

Ingredients:

For the Tacos:

- 1 lb (450g) of your choice of meat (such as beef skirt steak, pork shoulder, or chicken thighs)
- 2 tablespoons vegetable oil
- 1 tablespoon ground cumin
- 1 tablespoon chili powder
- 1 teaspoon smoked paprika
- 1 teaspoon garlic powder
- 1/2 teaspoon onion powder
- 1/2 teaspoon dried oregano
- Salt, to taste
- Freshly ground black pepper, to taste
- 12 small corn tortillas (or flour tortillas, if preferred)

For the Toppings:

- 1 cup chopped fresh cilantro
- 1 cup diced onion
- 1-2 limes, cut into wedges
- 1 cup diced tomatoes or Pico de Gallo (optional)
- 1-2 avocados, sliced or diced (optional)
- Salsa or hot sauce (optional)
- Radishes, thinly sliced (optional)

Instructions:

1. **Prepare the Meat:**
   - **Beef or Pork:** Slice the meat into thin strips (about 1/2 inch wide). If using pork shoulder, it may need to be cooked longer and shredded.
   - **Chicken:** Cut the chicken into small pieces or strips.
2. **Season and Cook the Meat:**
   - In a large bowl, combine the ground cumin, chili powder, smoked paprika, garlic powder, onion powder, dried oregano, salt, and pepper.
   - Add the meat and toss to coat evenly with the seasoning mix.
   - Heat the vegetable oil in a large skillet or grill pan over medium-high heat.
   - Add the seasoned meat to the skillet in a single layer. Cook, turning occasionally, until the meat is browned and cooked through. Beef or pork will take about 5-7 minutes; chicken will take about 7-10 minutes.
   - If using pork shoulder, cook until tender and easily shred with a fork.

3. **Warm the Tortillas:**
   - Heat the tortillas in a dry skillet over medium heat for about 30 seconds on each side, or until they are warm and pliable. Alternatively, you can wrap them in a damp paper towel and microwave them for about 30 seconds.
4. **Assemble the Tacos:**
   - Place a few spoonfuls of the cooked meat onto each tortilla.
   - Top with chopped cilantro, diced onion, and any other desired toppings like diced tomatoes, avocado, or radishes.
   - Squeeze a lime wedge over the top and add salsa or hot sauce if desired.
5. **Serve:**
   - Serve the tacos immediately while they are warm, accompanied by additional lime wedges and your favorite salsa.

Enjoy your delicious Mexican Street Tacos, bursting with authentic flavors and fresh toppings!

Chilaquiles

Ingredients:

For the Chilaquiles:

- 10-12 corn tortillas
- Vegetable oil (for frying)
- 2 cups of red or green salsa (see Salsa Verde or Enchilada Sauce recipes, or use store-bought)

For the Toppings:

- 1 cup shredded cheese (such as queso fresco, Monterey Jack, or Cheddar)
- 1/2 cup finely chopped onion
- 1/2 cup chopped fresh cilantro
- 1-2 avocados, sliced or diced
- 2-3 large eggs (optional, for topping)
- Sour cream or Mexican crema (optional)
- Salsa or Pico de Gallo (optional)
- Lime wedges (optional)

Instructions:

1. **Prepare the Tortilla Chips:**
   - **Cut the Tortillas:** Stack the tortillas and cut them into triangles or strips.
   - **Fry the Chips:** Heat about 1/2 inch of vegetable oil in a large skillet over medium-high heat. Working in batches, fry the tortilla pieces until they are crisp and golden brown, about 2-3 minutes per batch. Use a slotted spoon to transfer the chips to a paper towel-lined plate to drain. Season with a little salt while they're still warm.
2. **Prepare the Sauce:**
   - **Heat the Salsa:** In a separate large skillet or saucepan, heat the salsa over medium heat until it begins to simmer.
3. **Combine Chips and Sauce:**
   - **Add Chips to Sauce:** Once the salsa is simmering, gently add the fried tortilla chips to the skillet. Stir gently to coat the chips with the sauce. Cook for about 2-3 minutes, until the chips begin to soften but are still somewhat crisp. Be careful not to overcook, as the chips can become too soggy.
4. **Prepare the Eggs (Optional):**
   - **Cook the Eggs:** If you want to add eggs, you can fry them in a separate pan or cook them to your liking (scrambled, sunny-side-up, etc.).
5. **Serve the Chilaquiles:**

- **Plate and Garnish:** Transfer the chilaquiles to serving plates. Top with shredded cheese, chopped onion, and fresh cilantro.
    - **Add Optional Toppings:** Add avocado slices, a dollop of sour cream or Mexican crema, and any additional salsa or Pico de Gallo if desired.
    - **Add Eggs:** Place a cooked egg on top of each serving if using.
6. **Serve Immediately:**
    - **Garnish with Lime:** Serve with lime wedges on the side for a fresh squeeze of lime juice.

Enjoy your Chilaquiles, a flavorful and satisfying dish that's perfect for breakfast or brunch!

Carnitas Tacos

Ingredients:

For the Carnitas:

- 3-4 lbs (1.4-1.8 kg) pork shoulder or butt, cut into 2-inch chunks
- 1 tablespoon vegetable oil
- 1 large onion, chopped
- 4 cloves garlic, minced
- 1 cup orange juice
- 1/2 cup chicken or beef broth
- 2 tablespoons lime juice
- 1 tablespoon ground cumin
- 1 tablespoon dried oregano
- 1 teaspoon paprika
- 1/2 teaspoon cayenne pepper (optional, for heat)
- 1 bay leaf
- Salt, to taste
- Freshly ground black pepper, to taste

For the Tacos:

- 12 small corn or flour tortillas
- 1 cup finely chopped fresh cilantro
- 1 cup diced onion
- 1-2 limes, cut into wedges
- 1-2 avocados, sliced or diced
- Salsa or Pico de Gallo (optional)
- Pickled jalapeños (optional)

Instructions:

1. **Prepare the Carnitas:**
    - **Sear the Pork:** Heat the vegetable oil in a large Dutch oven or heavy-bottomed pot over medium-high heat. Add the pork chunks in batches (do not overcrowd) and sear on all sides until browned. Remove the pork and set aside.
    - **Cook the Aromatics:** In the same pot, add the chopped onion and cook until softened, about 5 minutes. Stir in the minced garlic and cook for another minute.
    - **Combine Ingredients:** Return the seared pork to the pot. Add the orange juice, chicken or beef broth, lime juice, ground cumin, dried oregano, paprika, cayenne pepper (if using), bay leaf, salt, and pepper. Stir to combine.

- **Simmer:** Bring the mixture to a simmer. Cover the pot and reduce the heat to low. Simmer for about 2-3 hours, or until the pork is very tender and easily shreds with a fork. Alternatively, you can cook it in a slow cooker on low for 6-8 hours.
2. **Shred the Pork:**
    - Once the pork is tender, remove it from the pot and shred it with two forks. Return the shredded pork to the pot and mix with the juices. If you prefer crispy carnitas, you can spread the shredded pork on a baking sheet and broil it for 5-10 minutes, or until the edges are crispy.
3. **Prepare the Tortillas:**
    - Warm the tortillas in a dry skillet over medium heat, or wrap them in a damp paper towel and microwave them for about 30 seconds until pliable.
4. **Assemble the Tacos:**
    - Place a generous amount of carnitas on each tortilla.
    - Top with chopped fresh cilantro, diced onion, and any additional toppings like avocado, salsa, or pickled jalapeños.
    - Squeeze a lime wedge over the top for added brightness.
5. **Serve:**
    - Serve the carnitas tacos immediately while warm, with extra lime wedges and salsa on the side.

Enjoy your flavorful and satisfying Carnitas Tacos!

Barbacoa Beef

Ingredients:

- 3-4 lbs (1.4-1.8 kg) beef chuck roast or brisket
- 2 tablespoons vegetable oil
- 1 large onion, chopped
- 4 cloves garlic, minced
- 2-3 dried guajillo or ancho chilies, stems and seeds removed (for a smoky flavor) or 2 tablespoons chili powder
- 1/4 cup apple cider vinegar
- 1/2 cup beef broth
- 1/4 cup lime juice (about 2 limes)
- 2 tablespoons tomato paste
- 1 tablespoon ground cumin
- 1 tablespoon dried oregano
- 1 teaspoon paprika
- 1/2 teaspoon ground cloves
- 1-2 bay leaves
- Salt, to taste
- Freshly ground black pepper, to taste
- 2 tablespoons brown sugar (optional, for a hint of sweetness)

Instructions:

1. **Prepare the Beef:**
    - **Sear the Beef:** Heat the vegetable oil in a large skillet or Dutch oven over medium-high heat. Season the beef with salt and pepper. Sear the beef on all sides until browned. Remove the beef from the skillet and set aside.
2. **Prepare the Sauce:**
    - **Toast the Chilies (if using):** In the same skillet, add the dried chilies and toast them for about 1-2 minutes until fragrant. Be careful not to burn them. Remove the chilies and place them in a bowl with enough hot water to cover them. Let them soak for about 10 minutes, then drain and blend them with a little of the soaking water to make a paste. If using chili powder, skip this step.
    - **Cook Aromatics:** In the same skillet, add the chopped onion and cook until softened, about 5 minutes. Stir in the minced garlic and cook for another minute.
    - **Combine Ingredients:** Stir in the tomato paste, apple cider vinegar, beef broth, lime juice, ground cumin, dried oregano, paprika, ground cloves, and brown sugar (if using). Add the chili paste (if using) and mix well.
3. **Slow Cook the Beef:**
    - **Add to Slow Cooker:** Place the seared beef in a slow cooker. Pour the prepared sauce over the beef and add the bay leaves.

- **Cook:** Cover and cook on low for 8-10 hours, or on high for 4-6 hours, until the beef is tender and easily shreds with a fork.
4. **Shred the Beef:**
    - **Shred:** Once the beef is tender, remove it from the slow cooker and shred it with two forks. Return the shredded beef to the slow cooker and mix with the juices.
5. **Serve:**
    - **Assemble:** Serve the barbacoa beef in tacos, burritos, or bowls. Top with your favorite toppings such as chopped cilantro, diced onions, lime wedges, salsa, and avocado.

Tips:

- **For Extra Flavor:** If you prefer a richer flavor, you can cook the beef in a Dutch oven or oven-safe pot at 300°F (150°C) for 3-4 hours instead of using a slow cooker.
- **Adjust Spice Level:** Adjust the amount of chili powder or chilies based on your heat preference.

Enjoy your tender and flavorful Barbacoa Beef!

Margarita Chicken

Ingredients:

For the Marinade:

- 1/4 cup tequila (optional, can be replaced with additional lime juice)
- 1/4 cup lime juice (about 2 limes)
- 1/4 cup olive oil
- 2 tablespoons orange juice
- 3 tablespoons honey or agave syrup
- 4 cloves garlic, minced
- 1 tablespoon chopped fresh cilantro (or 1 teaspoon dried cilantro)
- 1 teaspoon ground cumin
- 1 teaspoon smoked paprika
- 1/2 teaspoon chili powder
- 1/2 teaspoon salt
- Freshly ground black pepper, to taste

For the Chicken:

- 4 boneless, skinless chicken breasts or thighs
- Lime wedges and fresh cilantro, for garnish

Instructions:

1. **Prepare the Marinade:**
   - In a medium bowl, whisk together the tequila, lime juice, olive oil, orange juice, honey or agave syrup, minced garlic, chopped cilantro, ground cumin, smoked paprika, chili powder, salt, and black pepper until well combined.
2. **Marinate the Chicken:**
   - Place the chicken breasts or thighs in a resealable plastic bag or a shallow dish.
   - Pour the marinade over the chicken, making sure all pieces are evenly coated.
   - Seal the bag or cover the dish and refrigerate for at least 30 minutes, or up to 4 hours for maximum flavor.
3. **Cook the Chicken:**
   - **Grilling Method:** Preheat your grill to medium-high heat. Remove the chicken from the marinade and discard the marinade. Grill the chicken for 6-8 minutes per side, or until the internal temperature reaches 165°F (74°C) and the chicken is cooked through.
   - **Pan-Searing Method:** Heat a large skillet over medium-high heat with a little oil. Remove the chicken from the marinade and discard the marinade. Cook the chicken for 6-8 minutes per side, or until the internal temperature reaches 165°F (74°C) and the chicken is cooked through.

- **Baking Method:** Preheat your oven to 375°F (190°C). Remove the chicken from the marinade and discard the marinade. Place the chicken on a baking sheet and bake for 25-30 minutes, or until the internal temperature reaches 165°F (74°C) and the chicken is cooked through.

4. **Serve:**
   - Garnish the cooked chicken with lime wedges and fresh cilantro.
   - Serve with your favorite sides, such as rice, beans, or a fresh salad.

Tips:

- **Substitute Tequila:** If you prefer not to use tequila, you can replace it with extra lime juice or a splash of white wine.
- **For Extra Flavor:** Consider adding a splash of orange liqueur (like triple sec) for an additional layer of flavor.

Enjoy your tangy and delicious Margarita Chicken!

Cactus Salad (Nopales)

Ingredients:

- 4-5 nopal cactus pads (fresh or thawed if frozen)
- 1 tablespoon olive oil
- 1/2 small red onion, finely chopped
- 2 cloves garlic, minced
- 1 large tomato, diced
- 1/2 cup fresh cilantro, chopped
- 1-2 jalapeños, finely chopped (optional, for heat)
- Juice of 2 limes
- 1/4 cup crumbled queso fresco or feta cheese (optional)
- Salt, to taste
- Freshly ground black pepper, to taste

Instructions:

1. **Prepare the Nopales:**
   - **Clean the Nopales:** Using tongs or a fork, hold the cactus pads over an open flame or use a gas burner to char the pads lightly. This will help remove the thorns and slightly soften the pads. Alternatively, you can use a vegetable peeler to carefully remove the thorns.
   - **Peel and Slice:** Once the nopales are charred and cooled, peel off the skin with a knife or vegetable peeler. Cut the pads into small, thin strips or dice them.
2. **Cook the Nopales:**
   - Heat the olive oil in a skillet over medium heat.
   - Add the chopped nopal pads and cook for about 5-7 minutes, stirring occasionally, until they are tender and the sliminess has reduced. If there's excess liquid, cook until it evaporates.
   - Add the minced garlic and cook for an additional minute. Remove from heat and let cool.
3. **Combine the Salad Ingredients:**
   - In a large bowl, combine the cooked nopales, diced tomato, chopped red onion, chopped cilantro, and chopped jalapeños (if using).
   - Drizzle with lime juice and toss to combine. Season with salt and freshly ground black pepper to taste.
4. **Add Cheese (Optional):**
   - If desired, gently fold in the crumbled queso fresco or feta cheese.
5. **Serve:**
   - Serve the cactus salad immediately, or chill in the refrigerator for about 30 minutes to let the flavors meld.
   - This salad can be enjoyed on its own or as a topping for tacos, alongside grilled meats, or as part of a larger Mexican meal.

Tips:

- **To Make Ahead:** You can prepare the nopales and the salad ingredients ahead of time and store them separately in the refrigerator. Combine them just before serving to keep the salad fresh and crisp.
- **Substitute:** If fresh nopales are unavailable, you can use canned or jarred nopales, but be sure to rinse them thoroughly to remove excess brine.

Enjoy your refreshing and flavorful Cactus Salad!

Baked Mexican Chicken

Ingredients:

For the Chicken Marinade:

- 4 boneless, skinless chicken breasts (or thighs)
- 1/4 cup olive oil
- 1/4 cup lime juice (about 2 limes)
- 2 tablespoons chili powder
- 1 tablespoon ground cumin
- 1 tablespoon paprika
- 1 teaspoon garlic powder
- 1 teaspoon onion powder
- 1 teaspoon dried oregano
- 1/2 teaspoon cayenne pepper (optional, for heat)
- Salt, to taste
- Freshly ground black pepper, to taste

For the Topping:

- 1/2 cup shredded cheese (cheddar, Monterey Jack, or a Mexican blend)
- 1/4 cup breadcrumbs (optional, for extra crunch)
- 2 tablespoons chopped fresh cilantro (optional, for garnish)

Instructions:

1. **Marinate the Chicken:**
    - In a bowl, whisk together the olive oil, lime juice, chili powder, ground cumin, paprika, garlic powder, onion powder, dried oregano, cayenne pepper (if using), salt, and black pepper.
    - Place the chicken breasts or thighs in a resealable plastic bag or a shallow dish and pour the marinade over them. Ensure the chicken is evenly coated.
    - Seal the bag or cover the dish and refrigerate for at least 30 minutes, or up to 4 hours for deeper flavor.
2. **Prepare for Baking:**
    - Preheat your oven to 375°F (190°C).
    - Lightly grease a baking dish or line it with parchment paper.
3. **Bake the Chicken:**
    - Remove the chicken from the marinade and place it in the prepared baking dish. Discard the used marinade.
    - If using breadcrumbs, sprinkle them evenly over the top of each chicken piece for added crunch.

- Bake in the preheated oven for 25-30 minutes, or until the chicken reaches an internal temperature of 165°F (74°C) and is cooked through.
4. **Add Cheese (Optional):**
    - About 5 minutes before the chicken is done, sprinkle the shredded cheese over the top of each piece.
    - Return to the oven and bake until the cheese is melted and bubbly.
5. **Serve:**
    - Remove from the oven and let the chicken rest for a few minutes before serving.
    - Garnish with chopped fresh cilantro, if desired.

Serving Suggestions:

- Serve the baked Mexican chicken with a side of Mexican rice, black beans, or a fresh salad.
- Top with additional lime wedges, salsa, or guacamole for extra flavor.

Enjoy your flavorful and easy-to-make Baked Mexican Chicken!

Mexican Stuffed Peppers

Ingredients:

For the Filling:

- 4 large bell peppers (red, yellow, or green)
- 1 lb (450g) ground beef or ground turkey
- 1 cup cooked rice (white, brown, or Mexican rice)
- 1 can (15 oz) black beans, drained and rinsed
- 1 cup corn kernels (fresh, frozen, or canned)
- 1 cup diced tomatoes (canned or fresh)
- 1 small onion, diced
- 2 cloves garlic, minced
- 1 tablespoon chili powder
- 1 teaspoon ground cumin
- 1/2 teaspoon smoked paprika
- 1/2 teaspoon dried oregano
- Salt, to taste
- Freshly ground black pepper, to taste
- 1 cup shredded cheese (cheddar, Monterey Jack, or a Mexican blend)
- 2 tablespoons chopped fresh cilantro (optional, for garnish)

For the Peppers:

- 4 large bell peppers (any color)
- Olive oil (for drizzling)

Instructions:

1. **Prepare the Peppers:**
   - Preheat your oven to 375°F (190°C).
   - Cut the tops off the bell peppers and remove the seeds and membranes. If needed, trim the bottoms slightly to make them stable in the baking dish, but be careful not to cut through the bottom.
2. **Cook the Filling:**
   - Heat a large skillet over medium heat. Add the ground beef or turkey and cook until browned, breaking it up with a spoon as it cooks. Drain any excess fat.
   - Add the diced onion and cook for about 5 minutes until softened. Stir in the minced garlic and cook for another minute.
   - Add the cooked rice, black beans, corn, diced tomatoes, chili powder, ground cumin, smoked paprika, dried oregano, salt, and black pepper. Stir to combine and cook for an additional 5 minutes until everything is heated through and well mixed.

3. **Stuff the Peppers:**
    - Place the bell peppers in a baking dish.
    - Spoon the filling mixture into each pepper, packing it in tightly. If desired, top each pepper with a sprinkle of shredded cheese.
4. **Bake the Peppers:**
    - Drizzle the tops of the peppers with a little olive oil.
    - Cover the baking dish with aluminum foil and bake in the preheated oven for 25 minutes.
    - Remove the foil and bake for an additional 10-15 minutes, or until the peppers are tender and the cheese is melted and bubbly.
5. **Serve:**
    - Remove the peppers from the oven and let them cool slightly.
    - Garnish with chopped fresh cilantro if desired.

Serving Suggestions:

- Serve the stuffed peppers with a side of Mexican rice, guacamole, or a fresh salad.
- Top with additional salsa, sour cream, or avocado slices for extra flavor.

Enjoy your flavorful and hearty Mexican Stuffed Peppers!

Coconut Flan

Ingredients:

For the Caramel:

- 1 cup granulated sugar
- 1/4 cup water

For the Flan:

- 1 can (14 oz) sweetened condensed milk
- 1 can (13.5 oz) coconut milk
- 4 large eggs
- 1/2 cup granulated sugar
- 1 teaspoon vanilla extract
- 1/2 cup shredded coconut (sweetened or unsweetened)

Instructions:

1. **Prepare the Caramel:**
   - In a medium saucepan, combine the granulated sugar and water. Cook over medium heat, stirring occasionally, until the sugar dissolves.
   - Increase the heat to medium-high and cook without stirring until the mixture turns a deep amber color. Swirl the pan gently to ensure even caramelization. Be careful not to burn the caramel.
   - Immediately pour the caramel into the bottom of a 9-inch round cake pan or a flan mold, tilting the pan to coat the bottom evenly. Set aside to cool and harden.
2. **Prepare the Flan Mixture:**
   - Preheat your oven to 325°F (165°C).
   - In a large mixing bowl, whisk together the sweetened condensed milk, coconut milk, eggs, granulated sugar, and vanilla extract until smooth and well combined.
   - Stir in the shredded coconut.
3. **Bake the Flan:**
   - Pour the flan mixture over the set caramel in the prepared pan.
   - Place the pan in a larger baking dish or roasting pan. Fill the outer pan with hot water until it reaches halfway up the sides of the flan pan (this creates a water bath for even cooking).
   - Bake in the preheated oven for 50-60 minutes, or until the flan is set and a knife inserted into the center comes out clean.
4. **Cool and Unmold:**
   - Remove the flan from the water bath and let it cool to room temperature. Then refrigerate for at least 4 hours, or overnight, to chill and set completely.

- To unmold, run a knife around the edges of the flan to loosen it. Place a serving plate over the top of the pan and carefully invert the flan onto the plate. The caramel will flow over the top of the flan.
5. **Serve:**
    - Slice and serve chilled. Enjoy the rich, creamy texture and the sweet coconut flavor of your homemade Coconut Flan!

Tips:

- **For a Richer Flavor:** You can use coconut cream in place of some of the coconut milk for an even creamier texture.
- **Garnishing:** Optionally, garnish with additional shredded coconut or toasted coconut flakes before serving for added texture and flavor.

Enjoy your decadent and tropical Coconut Flan!

Tres Leches Cake

Ingredients:

For the Cake:

- 1 cup all-purpose flour
- 1 1/2 teaspoons baking powder
- 1/4 teaspoon salt
- 1/2 cup unsalted butter, room temperature
- 1 cup granulated sugar
- 5 large eggs
- 1 teaspoon vanilla extract
- 1/2 cup whole milk

For the Tres Leches Mixture:

- 1 can (14 oz) sweetened condensed milk
- 1 can (12 oz) evaporated milk
- 1 cup whole milk or heavy cream

For the Topping:

- 1 cup heavy cream
- 2 tablespoons granulated sugar
- 1 teaspoon vanilla extract
- Fresh fruit or berries for garnish (optional)

Instructions:

1. **Prepare the Cake:**
   - Preheat your oven to 350°F (175°C). Grease and flour a 9x13-inch baking pan or line it with parchment paper.
   - In a medium bowl, whisk together the flour, baking powder, and salt. Set aside.
   - In a large mixing bowl, cream together the butter and granulated sugar until light and fluffy.
   - Beat in the eggs one at a time, ensuring each is fully incorporated before adding the next. Stir in the vanilla extract.
   - Gradually add the dry ingredients to the butter mixture, alternating with the whole milk, beginning and ending with the dry ingredients. Mix until just combined.
   - Pour the batter into the prepared pan and spread evenly.
   - Bake in the preheated oven for 25-30 minutes, or until a toothpick inserted into the center of the cake comes out clean.
   - Allow the cake to cool completely in the pan on a wire rack.

2. **Prepare the Tres Leches Mixture:**
   - In a bowl or large measuring cup, whisk together the sweetened condensed milk, evaporated milk, and whole milk (or heavy cream) until well combined.
3. **Soak the Cake:**
   - Once the cake is completely cooled, use a fork or toothpick to poke holes all over the top of the cake.
   - Slowly pour the tres leches mixture over the cake, allowing it to soak in. Make sure to pour slowly so the cake absorbs the milk mixture evenly.
4. **Prepare the Topping:**
   - In a large mixing bowl, whip the heavy cream, granulated sugar, and vanilla extract until soft peaks form.
   - Spread the whipped cream evenly over the top of the soaked cake.
5. **Serve:**
   - Garnish with fresh fruit or berries if desired.
   - Chill the cake in the refrigerator for at least 2 hours before serving to allow the flavors to meld and the cake to fully absorb the milk mixture.

Tips:

- **For Extra Flavor:** You can add a splash of rum or vanilla extract to the tres leches mixture for added depth of flavor.
- **Garnishing:** Consider garnishing with fresh mint leaves or toasted coconut for additional decoration and flavor.

Enjoy your creamy and indulgent Tres Leches Cake!

Mexican Hot Chocolate

Ingredients:

- 2 cups whole milk (or any milk of your choice)
- 1/2 cup water
- 1/2 cup Mexican chocolate or semi-sweet chocolate, chopped (see tips below for substitutes)
- 1/4 cup sugar (adjust to taste)
- 1 cinnamon stick
- 1/4 teaspoon ground cinnamon
- 1/4 teaspoon vanilla extract
- A pinch of cayenne pepper or chili powder (optional, for a hint of spice)

Instructions:

1. **Heat the Liquids:**
   - In a medium saucepan, combine the milk and water. Heat over medium heat until warm, but not boiling.
2. **Add the Chocolate:**
   - Stir in the chopped Mexican chocolate or semi-sweet chocolate and continue to heat, stirring frequently, until the chocolate is completely melted and the mixture is smooth.
3. **Flavor the Hot Chocolate:**
   - Add the sugar, cinnamon stick, ground cinnamon, and vanilla extract. Stir until the sugar is dissolved and the flavors are well combined.
   - If using, add a pinch of cayenne pepper or chili powder for a subtle kick of heat. Stir well.
4. **Blend for Froth (Optional):**
   - For a traditional touch, you can use a molinillo (a traditional Mexican wooden whisk) to froth the hot chocolate. Alternatively, you can use a handheld frother or blender. Just blend the hot chocolate for a few seconds to create a frothy texture.
5. **Serve:**
   - Remove the cinnamon stick before serving.
   - Pour the hot chocolate into mugs and serve immediately.

Tips:

- **Mexican Chocolate:** Mexican chocolate, such as Abuelita or Ibarra, is traditionally used in this recipe. It has a distinct flavor with hints of cinnamon and sometimes almonds. If you don't have Mexican chocolate, you can use semi-sweet chocolate and add a bit of extra cinnamon.

- **Adjusting Sweetness:** Adjust the amount of sugar based on your taste and the sweetness of the chocolate you're using.
- **For a Richer Flavor:** You can use whole milk or a mixture of milk and cream for a richer texture.

Enjoy your warm and comforting Mexican Hot Chocolate!

Mexican Shrimp Cocktail

Ingredients:

- 1 lb (450g) large shrimp, peeled and deveined
- 1/2 cup ketchup
- 1/2 cup clam juice (or seafood stock)
- 1/4 cup freshly squeezed lime juice (about 2 limes)
- 1/4 cup freshly squeezed orange juice (about 1 orange)
- 1/4 cup finely chopped red onion
- 1 medium tomato, diced
- 1/2 cup diced cucumber
- 1/4 cup chopped fresh cilantro
- 1 small jalapeño or serrano pepper, finely chopped (optional, for heat)
- 1 avocado, diced (optional, for garnish)
- Salt and freshly ground black pepper, to taste
- Lime wedges, for serving

Instructions:

1. **Cook the Shrimp:**
   - In a large pot, bring water to a boil and add a pinch of salt. Add the shrimp and cook for 2-3 minutes, or until the shrimp are pink and opaque.
   - Drain the shrimp and immediately transfer them to a bowl of ice water to stop the cooking process. Once cooled, drain again and pat dry with paper towels. Chop the shrimp into bite-sized pieces.
2. **Prepare the Cocktail Sauce:**
   - In a large bowl, whisk together the ketchup, clam juice, lime juice, and orange juice until well combined.
3. **Combine Ingredients:**
   - Add the chopped shrimp, diced tomato, diced cucumber, chopped red onion, cilantro, and finely chopped jalapeño (if using) to the cocktail sauce. Mix well.
   - Season with salt and freshly ground black pepper to taste. Adjust seasoning as needed.
4. **Chill and Serve:**
   - Cover the bowl and refrigerate the shrimp cocktail for at least 30 minutes to allow the flavors to meld and the cocktail to chill.
   - Before serving, gently fold in the diced avocado if using.
5. **Garnish and Enjoy:**
   - Serve the shrimp cocktail in individual bowls or glasses.
   - Garnish with additional cilantro and lime wedges on the side.

Tips:

- **For Extra Flavor:** You can add a splash of hot sauce or a bit of diced fresh chili if you like more heat.
- **Serving Suggestion:** This dish pairs well with tortilla chips or crispy tostadas for added crunch.

Enjoy your refreshing and flavorful Mexican Shrimp Cocktail!

Churros

Ingredients:

For the Churros:

- 1 cup water
- 1/2 cup unsalted butter
- 1/4 teaspoon salt
- 1 tablespoon granulated sugar
- 1 cup all-purpose flour
- 3 large eggs
- 1 teaspoon vanilla extract

For the Cinnamon Sugar Coating:

- 1/2 cup granulated sugar
- 1 tablespoon ground cinnamon

For Frying:

- Vegetable oil (for frying)

For Optional Chocolate Sauce:

- 1/2 cup heavy cream
- 4 oz semi-sweet chocolate, chopped
- 1 tablespoon granulated sugar (optional)
- 1/2 teaspoon vanilla extract (optional)

Instructions:

1. **Prepare the Dough:**
   - In a medium saucepan, combine the water, butter, salt, and granulated sugar. Heat over medium heat until the butter is melted and the mixture comes to a boil.
   - Remove from heat and stir in the flour all at once. Continue to stir until the dough comes together and pulls away from the sides of the pan.
   - Let the dough cool for about 5 minutes. Once cooled slightly, beat in the eggs one at a time, mixing well after each addition. Stir in the vanilla extract. The dough should be smooth and slightly sticky.
2. **Prepare the Cinnamon Sugar Coating:**
   - In a shallow dish, mix together the granulated sugar and ground cinnamon. Set aside.
3. **Heat the Oil:**

- Heat about 2 inches of vegetable oil in a large, heavy-bottomed pot or deep fryer to 350°F (175°C). Use a thermometer to ensure the oil is at the correct temperature.

4. **Pipe the Churros:**
   - Fit a large piping bag with a star-shaped tip (or use a churro maker if you have one). Fill the piping bag with the churro dough.
   - Pipe strips of dough (about 4-6 inches long) directly into the hot oil, cutting them off with scissors or a knife. Fry in batches to avoid overcrowding, and cook until golden brown and crispy, about 2-3 minutes per side. Use a slotted spoon to remove the churros and drain on paper towels.

5. **Coat with Cinnamon Sugar:**
   - While the churros are still warm, roll them in the cinnamon sugar mixture until well coated.

6. **Prepare Optional Chocolate Sauce (If Desired):**
   - In a small saucepan, heat the heavy cream over medium heat until just about to boil. Remove from heat and add the chopped chocolate. Stir until smooth and melted. Add sugar and vanilla extract if using.

7. **Serve:**
   - Serve the churros warm with the chocolate sauce on the side for dipping, or enjoy them on their own.

Tips:

- **Oil Temperature:** Maintaining the correct oil temperature is crucial for crispy churros. If the oil is too hot, the churros will cook too quickly on the outside and remain raw inside. If it's too cool, they will absorb more oil and become greasy.
- **Dough Consistency:** The dough should be thick enough to hold its shape when piped but not so thick that it's difficult to pipe.

Enjoy your homemade churros with a warm chocolate dipping sauce or simply as they are!

Spicy Black Beans

Ingredients:

- 2 cans (15 oz each) black beans, drained and rinsed (or 3 cups cooked black beans)
- 1 tablespoon olive oil
- 1 medium onion, finely chopped
- 3 cloves garlic, minced
- 1 jalapeño or serrano pepper, finely chopped (seeds removed for less heat)
- 1 teaspoon ground cumin
- 1 teaspoon smoked paprika
- 1/2 teaspoon chili powder
- 1/2 teaspoon dried oregano
- 1/2 cup tomato sauce or diced tomatoes
- 1/4 cup vegetable or chicken broth
- 1 tablespoon lime juice
- Salt, to taste
- Freshly ground black pepper, to taste
- 2 tablespoons chopped fresh cilantro (optional, for garnish)

Instructions:

1. **Sauté the Aromatics:**
    - Heat the olive oil in a large skillet or saucepan over medium heat.
    - Add the chopped onion and cook for about 5 minutes, or until softened and translucent.
    - Stir in the minced garlic and chopped jalapeño (or serrano pepper). Cook for an additional 1-2 minutes until fragrant.
2. **Add the Spices:**
    - Add the ground cumin, smoked paprika, chili powder, and dried oregano to the skillet. Stir well to coat the onions and peppers with the spices.
3. **Combine the Beans and Sauce:**
    - Add the drained and rinsed black beans, tomato sauce (or diced tomatoes), and vegetable or chicken broth to the skillet. Stir to combine and bring to a simmer.
4. **Simmer and Season:**
    - Reduce the heat to low and let the beans simmer for about 10-15 minutes, or until they are heated through and the flavors have melded together.
    - Stir in the lime juice and season with salt and freshly ground black pepper to taste.
5. **Garnish and Serve:**
    - Garnish with chopped fresh cilantro if desired.
    - Serve hot as a side dish or as a topping for tacos, burritos, or salads.

Tips:

- **Adjust Spice Level:** If you prefer a milder dish, omit the jalapeño or serrano pepper, or use only half. For extra heat, add more chili powder or a splash of hot sauce.
- **Make Ahead:** These beans can be made ahead of time and stored in the refrigerator for up to 4 days. They also freeze well for up to 3 months.

Enjoy your spicy and flavorful black beans!

Tortilla Soup

Ingredients:

For the Soup:

- 2 tablespoons olive oil
- 1 medium onion, diced
- 3 cloves garlic, minced
- 1 jalapeño or serrano pepper, seeded and diced (optional, for heat)
- 1 teaspoon ground cumin
- 1 teaspoon chili powder
- 1/2 teaspoon smoked paprika
- 1/2 teaspoon dried oregano
- 1 can (14.5 oz) diced tomatoes
- 4 cups chicken or vegetable broth
- 1 cup cooked chicken, shredded (or use a rotisserie chicken)
- 1 cup frozen or fresh corn kernels
- 1 can (15 oz) black beans, drained and rinsed
- 1 cup cooked rice (optional)
- Salt and freshly ground black pepper, to taste
- 1 tablespoon lime juice (about 1 lime)

For the Tortilla Strips:

- 6 small corn tortillas, cut into thin strips
- 2 tablespoons vegetable oil
- Salt, to taste

Toppings (optional):

- 1 avocado, diced
- 1/2 cup shredded cheese (cheddar, Monterey Jack, or Mexican blend)
- 1/4 cup chopped fresh cilantro
- 1/2 cup sour cream
- Lime wedges
- Sliced radishes
- Chopped green onions

Instructions:

1. **Prepare the Tortilla Strips:**
    - Preheat the oven to 375°F (190°C).

- Place the tortilla strips on a baking sheet in a single layer. Drizzle with vegetable oil and toss to coat evenly.
- Bake for 10-15 minutes, or until crispy and golden brown. Remove from the oven and season with salt. Set aside.

2. **Cook the Soup Base:**
   - Heat olive oil in a large pot or Dutch oven over medium heat.
   - Add the diced onion and cook for about 5 minutes, or until softened and translucent.
   - Stir in the minced garlic and diced jalapeño (if using) and cook for another 1-2 minutes until fragrant.
   - Add the ground cumin, chili powder, smoked paprika, and dried oregano. Stir well to combine.
3. **Add Tomatoes and Broth:**
   - Pour in the diced tomatoes with their juices and cook for about 2 minutes.
   - Add the chicken or vegetable broth and bring to a simmer.
4. **Add the Remaining Ingredients:**
   - Stir in the shredded cooked chicken, corn kernels, black beans, and cooked rice (if using). Simmer for about 10 minutes, or until heated through.
   - Season with salt and freshly ground black pepper to taste.
   - Stir in the lime juice just before serving.
5. **Serve:**
   - Ladle the soup into bowls and top with crispy tortilla strips.
   - Add any desired toppings such as diced avocado, shredded cheese, chopped cilantro, sour cream, lime wedges, sliced radishes, and chopped green onions.

Tips:

- **Customize Your Soup:** Feel free to add other vegetables like bell peppers or zucchini for extra flavor and nutrition.
- **Make Ahead:** This soup can be made ahead and stored in the refrigerator for up to 3 days. Reheat before serving and add the tortilla strips just before serving to maintain their crispiness.

Enjoy your comforting and flavorful Tortilla Soup!

Mexican Cornbread

Ingredients:

- 1 cup cornmeal
- 1 cup all-purpose flour
- 1/4 cup granulated sugar
- 1 tablespoon baking powder
- 1/2 teaspoon salt
- 1/2 teaspoon ground cumin
- 1/2 teaspoon smoked paprika
- 1/4 teaspoon cayenne pepper (optional, for extra heat)
- 1 cup buttermilk (or use regular milk with 1 tablespoon lemon juice or vinegar)
- 1/2 cup unsalted butter, melted
- 2 large eggs
- 1 cup shredded cheddar cheese (or Mexican blend cheese)
- 1/2 cup finely chopped fresh cilantro
- 1-2 jalapeños, seeded and finely chopped (adjust to taste)
- 1 cup corn kernels (fresh, frozen, or canned)

Instructions:

1. **Preheat Oven:**
   - Preheat your oven to 400°F (200°C).
   - Grease an 8-inch square baking dish or a similar-sized oven-safe skillet.
2. **Mix Dry Ingredients:**
   - In a large mixing bowl, whisk together the cornmeal, flour, sugar, baking powder, salt, ground cumin, smoked paprika, and cayenne pepper (if using).
3. **Combine Wet Ingredients:**
   - In another bowl, whisk together the buttermilk, melted butter, and eggs until well combined.
4. **Combine Dry and Wet Ingredients:**
   - Pour the wet ingredients into the dry ingredients and stir until just combined. Be careful not to overmix.
5. **Add Mix-Ins:**
   - Gently fold in the shredded cheese, chopped cilantro, finely chopped jalapeños, and corn kernels.
6. **Bake:**
   - Pour the batter into the prepared baking dish or skillet, spreading it evenly.
   - Bake in the preheated oven for 25-30 minutes, or until the cornbread is golden brown and a toothpick inserted into the center comes out clean.
7. **Cool and Serve:**
   - Allow the cornbread to cool slightly before cutting into squares or wedges.

- Serve warm with butter, or as a side dish to your favorite Mexican meals.

Tips:

- **For Extra Moisture:** You can add a bit of creamed corn or sour cream to the batter for extra moisture and richness.
- **Adjust Spice Level:** If you prefer less heat, reduce or omit the jalapeños and cayenne pepper.
- **Serve With:** This cornbread pairs well with chili, soups, or as a side to dishes like tacos or enchiladas.

Enjoy your flavorful and spicy Mexican Cornbread!

Salsa Roja

Ingredients:

- 6 medium ripe tomatoes
- 1 small onion, peeled and quartered
- 2 cloves garlic, peeled
- 1-2 jalapeño or serrano peppers (adjust to taste)
- 1 tablespoon vegetable oil
- 1/4 cup fresh cilantro, chopped
- 1 tablespoon lime juice (about 1 lime)
- Salt, to taste
- Freshly ground black pepper, to taste

Instructions:

1. **Roast the Vegetables:**
    - Preheat your oven to 400°F (200°C).
    - Place the tomatoes, onion, garlic, and jalapeño (or serrano peppers) on a baking sheet.
    - Roast in the preheated oven for about 20-25 minutes, or until the tomatoes are soft and slightly charred, and the peppers have blackened skin. You can also use a broiler for a quicker roasting method; just keep an eye on the vegetables to prevent burning.
2. **Blend the Salsa:**
    - Remove the vegetables from the oven and let them cool slightly.
    - Transfer the roasted tomatoes, onion, garlic, and peppers to a blender or food processor. Blend until smooth. If you prefer a chunkier salsa, blend until just combined but still a bit chunky.
    - Add the vegetable oil, cilantro, and lime juice. Blend again to combine.
3. **Season:**
    - Taste the salsa and season with salt and freshly ground black pepper to taste. Adjust the heat level by adding more jalapeños or serrano peppers if desired.
4. **Chill and Serve:**
    - Transfer the salsa to a bowl and let it sit for at least 30 minutes to allow the flavors to meld together. You can also refrigerate it for up to a week.
    - Serve with tortilla chips, or as a topping for tacos, burritos, or grilled meats.

Tips:

- **For Extra Smokiness:** Add a chipotle pepper in adobo sauce to the blender for a smoky flavor.

- **Adjusting Consistency:** If the salsa is too thick, add a little bit of water to reach your desired consistency.

Enjoy your homemade Salsa Roja!

Chicken Pozole

Ingredients:

For the Soup:

- 2 tablespoons vegetable oil
- 1 medium onion, diced
- 3 cloves garlic, minced
- 1 tablespoon ground cumin
- 1 teaspoon dried oregano
- 1/2 teaspoon smoked paprika
- 1/2 teaspoon chili powder
- 1/4 teaspoon cayenne pepper (optional, for extra heat)
- 6 cups chicken broth
- 2 cups cooked, shredded chicken (such as rotisserie chicken or poached chicken breasts)
- 2 cans (15 oz each) hominy, drained and rinsed (or about 4 cups homemade hominy)
- 1-2 cans (4 oz each) diced green chilies (optional, for additional flavor and heat)
- Salt and freshly ground black pepper, to taste
- 1 tablespoon lime juice (about 1 lime)

For Garnishing:

- Shredded lettuce or cabbage
- Diced radishes
- Sliced jalapeños
- Chopped fresh cilantro
- Diced avocado
- Lime wedges
- Crumbled queso fresco or shredded cheese
- Tortilla chips or fried tortilla strips

Instructions:

1. **Prepare the Base:**
   - Heat the vegetable oil in a large pot or Dutch oven over medium heat.
   - Add the diced onion and cook for about 5 minutes, or until softened and translucent.
   - Stir in the minced garlic and cook for another 1-2 minutes until fragrant.
2. **Add the Spices:**
   - Add the ground cumin, dried oregano, smoked paprika, chili powder, and cayenne pepper (if using) to the pot. Stir well to combine and toast the spices for about 1 minute.

3. **Build the Soup:**
    - Pour in the chicken broth and bring to a boil.
    - Add the shredded chicken, hominy, and diced green chilies (if using). Reduce the heat and let the soup simmer for about 15-20 minutes, or until the flavors meld together and the hominy is heated through.
4. **Season and Finish:**
    - Stir in the lime juice and season with salt and freshly ground black pepper to taste.
5. **Serve:**
    - Ladle the pozole into bowls.
    - Garnish with shredded lettuce or cabbage, diced radishes, sliced jalapeños, chopped fresh cilantro, diced avocado, and crumbled queso fresco or shredded cheese.
    - Serve with tortilla chips or fried tortilla strips on the side for added crunch.

Tips:

- **For Extra Flavor:** You can add a splash of hot sauce or a few dashes of your favorite hot sauce to the soup if you like extra heat.
- **Homemade Hominy:** If using homemade hominy, make sure it's well-cooked before adding it to the soup.

Enjoy your hearty and flavorful Chicken Pozole!

El Pastor Marinade

Ingredients:

- 4-6 dried guajillo chiles
- 2 dried ancho chiles
- 1/4 cup apple cider vinegar
- 1/4 cup orange juice
- 1/4 cup pineapple juice
- 4 cloves garlic, minced
- 1 tablespoon ground cumin
- 1 tablespoon dried oregano
- 1 tablespoon smoked paprika
- 1 teaspoon ground coriander
- 1/2 teaspoon ground cinnamon
- 1/4 teaspoon ground cloves
- 1-2 tablespoons adobo sauce from a can of chipotle peppers in adobo (optional, for extra heat and smokiness)
- 1 tablespoon salt
- 2 tablespoons brown sugar or honey
- 2 tablespoons vegetable oil

Instructions:

1. **Prepare the Chiles:**
    - Remove the stems and seeds from the dried guajillo and ancho chiles.
    - Heat a dry skillet over medium heat and toast the chiles for about 1-2 minutes on each side, or until they become fragrant. Be careful not to burn them.
2. **Rehydrate the Chiles:**
    - Place the toasted chiles in a bowl and cover them with hot water. Let them soak for about 15 minutes, or until they are softened.
    - Drain the chiles and place them in a blender or food processor.
3. **Make the Marinade:**
    - To the blender, add the apple cider vinegar, orange juice, pineapple juice, minced garlic, ground cumin, dried oregano, smoked paprika, ground coriander, ground cinnamon, ground cloves, adobo sauce (if using), salt, brown sugar (or honey), and vegetable oil.
    - Blend until smooth, scraping down the sides as needed. The marinade should be thick and well combined.
4. **Marinate the Pork:**
    - Place the pork (typically pork shoulder or pork loin, thinly sliced) in a large bowl or resealable plastic bag.
    - Pour the marinade over the pork and toss to coat evenly.

- Cover the bowl or seal the bag and refrigerate for at least 4 hours, preferably overnight, to allow the flavors to penetrate the meat.

5. **Cook the Pork:**
   - Preheat your grill or a skillet over medium-high heat.
   - Cook the marinated pork slices until they are well browned and cooked through, about 4-5 minutes per side.
   - Slice the pork into thin strips and serve with warm tortillas, along with your favorite taco toppings like chopped onions, cilantro, pineapple, and salsa.

Tips:

- **Adjusting Heat:** If you prefer a milder marinade, omit the adobo sauce or use less. For extra heat, add more of the adobo sauce or some chopped fresh chilies.
- **Texture:** For a more authentic texture, you can skewer the marinated pork and cook it on a vertical rotisserie (trompo) or roast it in the oven with a similar effect.

Enjoy your delicious El Pastor tacos!

Taco Salad

Ingredients:

For the Salad:

- 1 lb (450g) ground beef or ground turkey
- 1 tablespoon olive oil
- 1 small onion, diced
- 2 cloves garlic, minced
- 1 packet taco seasoning mix (or homemade taco seasoning)
- 1/2 cup water (as required by taco seasoning instructions)
- 6 cups chopped romaine lettuce
- 1 cup cherry tomatoes, halved
- 1 cup diced cucumber
- 1 cup black beans, drained and rinsed
- 1 cup corn kernels (fresh, frozen, or canned)
- 1 avocado, diced
- 1 cup shredded cheddar cheese (or Mexican blend cheese)
- 1/2 cup sliced black olives (optional)
- 1/2 cup sliced radishes (optional)

For the Dressing:

- 1/2 cup sour cream
- 1/4 cup mayonnaise
- 1 tablespoon lime juice (about 1 lime)
- 1 tablespoon taco seasoning mix (or adjust to taste)
- Salt and freshly ground black pepper, to taste

For Garnish:

- Tortilla chips, crushed
- Fresh cilantro, chopped

Instructions:

1. **Prepare the Taco Meat:**
    - Heat olive oil in a large skillet over medium heat.
    - Add the diced onion and cook for about 5 minutes, or until softened and translucent.
    - Stir in the minced garlic and cook for another 1-2 minutes.
    - Add the ground beef or turkey and cook until browned and fully cooked, breaking it up with a spoon as it cooks.

- Drain any excess fat, if necessary.
- Stir in the taco seasoning mix and water, and simmer for about 5 minutes, or until the mixture thickens. Remove from heat and let cool slightly.

2. **Prepare the Dressing:**
   - In a bowl, whisk together the sour cream, mayonnaise, lime juice, taco seasoning mix, salt, and freshly ground black pepper until smooth. Adjust seasoning to taste.

3. **Assemble the Salad:**
   - In a large salad bowl, combine the chopped romaine lettuce, cherry tomatoes, diced cucumber, black beans, corn, diced avocado, shredded cheese, sliced black olives (if using), and sliced radishes (if using).
   - Add the slightly cooled taco meat on top.

4. **Dress and Toss:**
   - Drizzle the dressing over the salad and toss gently to combine all ingredients evenly.

5. **Garnish and Serve:**
   - Top the salad with crushed tortilla chips and a sprinkle of fresh cilantro.
   - Serve immediately, or refrigerate the salad components separately and combine just before serving to maintain freshness and crunch.

Tips:

- **Variations:** Feel free to add other toppings like sliced jalapeños, diced bell peppers, or pickled onions for extra flavor.
- **For a Lighter Version:** Use Greek yogurt instead of sour cream, and light mayonnaise.
- **Make-Ahead:** Prepare the taco meat and dressing in advance, and store them separately from the salad ingredients to keep everything fresh.

Enjoy your flavorful and satisfying Taco Salad!

Huaraches

Ingredients:

For the Huaraches:

- 2 cups masa harina (corn flour for tortillas)
- 1 1/4 cups warm water (or as needed)
- 1/2 teaspoon salt
- 1 tablespoon vegetable oil

For the Toppings:

- 1 cup refried beans (or black beans)
- 1 cup cooked and seasoned meat (such as beef, pork, or chicken), shredded or sliced
- 1 cup salsa verde or salsa roja
- 1/2 cup crumbled queso fresco or shredded cheese
- 1/2 cup thinly sliced lettuce or shredded cabbage
- 1/4 cup diced onions
- 1/4 cup chopped fresh cilantro
- 1 avocado, sliced
- Lime wedges, for serving
- Salsa or hot sauce, for extra heat (optional)

Instructions:

1. **Prepare the Huarache Dough:**
    - In a large mixing bowl, combine the masa harina and salt.
    - Gradually add the warm water, mixing with your hands until a smooth dough forms. The dough should be soft but not sticky. If too dry, add a bit more water; if too sticky, add a little more masa harina.
    - Divide the dough into 8-10 equal portions and shape each portion into a ball.
2. **Shape the Huaraches:**
    - On a piece of plastic wrap or parchment paper, flatten each dough ball into an oval shape using a tortilla press or your hands. The huaraches should be about 1/4 inch thick and 4-6 inches long.
    - To shape the huaraches, use your fingers to create a raised edge around the perimeter of each oval, forming a small rim.
3. **Cook the Huaraches:**
    - Heat a large skillet or griddle over medium-high heat. You can lightly oil the surface if desired.
    - Cook each huarache for about 1-2 minutes on each side, or until lightly browned and cooked through. The huaraches should have a slightly crispy exterior but remain soft inside. Transfer to a plate lined with paper towels to cool slightly.

4. **Assemble the Huaraches:**
    - Spread a layer of refried beans over each cooked huarache.
    - Top with the cooked and seasoned meat.
    - Spoon over some salsa verde or salsa roja.
    - Sprinkle with crumbled queso fresco or shredded cheese.
    - Add a layer of sliced lettuce or shredded cabbage.
    - Top with diced onions and chopped fresh cilantro.
    - Garnish with sliced avocado.
5. **Serve:**
    - Serve the huaraches with lime wedges and additional salsa or hot sauce on the side if desired.

Tips:

- **Toppings:** Customize your huaraches with additional toppings such as pickled jalapeños, radishes, or sour cream.
- **Making Ahead:** You can prepare the huarache dough and toppings in advance. Cook the huaraches and store them in an airtight container, then reheat them in a skillet before adding toppings.

Enjoy your homemade huaraches with your favorite toppings and sides!

Mexican Pizza

Ingredients:

For the Pizza Base:

- 4 large flour tortillas (or 6-8 small tortillas)
- 2 tablespoons vegetable oil (for brushing)
- 1 cup refried beans (or black beans, mashed)
- 1 cup salsa or taco sauce

For the Toppings:

- 1 cup cooked ground beef or shredded chicken (seasoned with taco seasoning)
- 1 cup shredded cheddar cheese (or Mexican blend cheese)
- 1 cup diced tomatoes
- 1/2 cup sliced black olives (optional)
- 1/2 cup sliced jalapeños (optional)
- 1/2 cup thinly sliced red onions
- 1/2 cup corn kernels (fresh, frozen, or canned)

For Garnishing:

- 1/2 cup chopped fresh cilantro
- 1 avocado, sliced
- 1/2 cup sour cream
- Lime wedges
- Sliced radishes (optional)
- Additional salsa or hot sauce

Instructions:

1. **Prepare the Tortillas:**
    - Preheat your oven to 400°F (200°C).
    - Brush each tortilla lightly with vegetable oil on both sides.
    - Place the tortillas on a baking sheet in a single layer. Bake for about 5 minutes, or until they start to crisp up but are still pliable.
2. **Assemble the Pizza:**
    - Remove the partially baked tortillas from the oven.
    - Spread a layer of refried beans on each tortilla.
    - Top with a spoonful of salsa or taco sauce, spreading it evenly over the beans.
    - Add a layer of cooked ground beef or shredded chicken.
    - Sprinkle with shredded cheese.
3. **Add Additional Toppings:**

- Top with diced tomatoes, sliced black olives, sliced jalapeños, thinly sliced red onions, and corn kernels.
4. **Bake the Pizza:**
    - Return the assembled pizzas to the oven and bake for an additional 10-12 minutes, or until the cheese is melted and bubbly, and the tortillas are crispy.
5. **Garnish and Serve:**
    - Remove the pizzas from the oven and let them cool slightly.
    - Garnish with chopped fresh cilantro, avocado slices, and a dollop of sour cream.
    - Serve with lime wedges and additional salsa or hot sauce on the side.

Tips:

- **Customize Toppings:** Feel free to customize your Mexican pizza with other toppings like pickled jalapeños, sliced bell peppers, or black beans.
- **For Extra Crispiness:** If you like extra crispy edges, bake the tortillas a bit longer before adding the toppings.
- **Make-Ahead:** Prepare the toppings and refried beans ahead of time, then assemble and bake the pizzas just before serving.

Enjoy your delicious and easy-to-make Mexican Pizza!

Tinga de Pollo

Ingredients:

- 2 lbs (900g) boneless, skinless chicken breasts or thighs
- 2 tablespoons vegetable oil
- 1 medium onion, finely chopped
- 3 cloves garlic, minced
- 2-3 dried pasilla chiles or ancho chiles (or 2 tablespoons of chili powder as a substitute)
- 1 can (14.5 oz) diced tomatoes
- 1/2 cup tomato sauce
- 1/2 cup chicken broth
- 1 tablespoon smoked paprika
- 1 teaspoon dried oregano
- 1 teaspoon ground cumin
- 1 bay leaf
- 1-2 tablespoons adobo sauce (from a can of chipotle peppers in adobo, optional, for extra smokiness)
- Salt and freshly ground black pepper, to taste
- 1 tablespoon vegetable oil (for frying the sauce)

For Serving:

- Corn or flour tortillas
- Shredded lettuce or cabbage
- Sliced avocados
- Crumbled queso fresco or shredded cheese
- Fresh cilantro, chopped
- Lime wedges
- Salsa or hot sauce

Instructions:

1. **Cook the Chicken:**
    - In a large pot, add the chicken breasts or thighs and cover with water. Season with a little salt.
    - Bring to a boil, then reduce the heat and simmer for about 20-25 minutes, or until the chicken is cooked through and tender.
    - Remove the chicken from the pot and let it cool slightly. Shred the chicken into bite-sized pieces using two forks or your hands. Set aside.
2. **Prepare the Chiles:**

- If using dried chiles, remove the stems and seeds. Toast the chiles in a dry skillet over medium heat for about 1-2 minutes, or until fragrant. Be careful not to burn them.
- Place the toasted chiles in a bowl and cover with hot water. Let them soak for about 10 minutes, or until softened.
- Drain the chiles and blend them with the can of diced tomatoes and tomato sauce until smooth.

3. **Make the Sauce:**
   - In a large skillet or saucepan, heat 2 tablespoons of vegetable oil over medium heat.
   - Add the finely chopped onion and cook until softened and translucent, about 5 minutes.
   - Stir in the minced garlic and cook for another 1-2 minutes.
   - Pour in the blended tomato and chile mixture. Add the chicken broth, smoked paprika, dried oregano, ground cumin, and bay leaf. Stir well to combine.
   - Bring the sauce to a simmer and cook for about 10 minutes, or until it thickens slightly.

4. **Combine Chicken with Sauce:**
   - Add the shredded chicken to the sauce and stir to coat well.
   - If using, add the adobo sauce for extra smokiness.
   - Simmer for an additional 10-15 minutes, or until the chicken is well-coated and heated through. Season with salt and freshly ground black pepper to taste.

5. **Serve:**
   - Serve the Tinga de Pollo with warm tortillas, or use it as a filling for tacos or tostadas.
   - Garnish with shredded lettuce or cabbage, sliced avocados, crumbled queso fresco, chopped fresh cilantro, and lime wedges.
   - Add salsa or hot sauce if desired.

Tips:

- **Adjusting Heat:** If you prefer a milder dish, omit the adobo sauce or use fewer chiles.
- **Make-Ahead:** Tinga de Pollo can be made ahead of time and stored in the refrigerator for up to 3 days. It also freezes well for up to 3 months.

Enjoy your delicious and spicy Tinga de Pollo!

Puerco en Salsa Verde

Ingredients:

For the Salsa Verde:

- 1 lb (450g) tomatillos, husked and rinsed
- 2-3 jalapeños or serrano chiles (adjust to taste)
- 1 small onion, quartered
- 2 cloves garlic, peeled
- 1/2 cup fresh cilantro, chopped
- 1 tablespoon lime juice (about 1 lime)
- Salt, to taste

For the Pork Stew:

- 2 lbs (900g) pork shoulder or pork loin, cut into bite-sized chunks
- 2 tablespoons vegetable oil
- 1 small onion, finely chopped
- 3 cloves garlic, minced
- 1 cup chicken broth
- 1/2 cup salsa verde (prepared)
- 1 teaspoon ground cumin
- 1 teaspoon dried oregano
- 1 bay leaf
- Salt and freshly ground black pepper, to taste

For Serving:

- Warm tortillas
- Rice and beans
- Sliced radishes
- Chopped fresh cilantro
- Lime wedges

Instructions:

1. **Prepare the Salsa Verde:**
    - Preheat your oven's broiler or a grill to high heat.
    - Place the tomatillos, jalapeños, onion, and garlic on a baking sheet. Broil or grill for about 5-7 minutes, turning occasionally, until the tomatillos and peppers are charred and softened.
    - Transfer the roasted tomatillos, jalapeños, onion, and garlic to a blender or food processor. Blend until smooth.

- Stir in the chopped cilantro, lime juice, and salt to taste. Set aside.
2. **Cook the Pork:**
    - Heat the vegetable oil in a large pot or Dutch oven over medium-high heat.
    - Add the pork chunks and cook until browned on all sides, about 5-7 minutes. Remove the pork and set aside.
    - In the same pot, add the finely chopped onion and cook until softened and translucent, about 5 minutes.
    - Stir in the minced garlic and cook for another 1-2 minutes.
3. **Simmer the Stew:**
    - Return the browned pork to the pot.
    - Add the chicken broth, salsa verde, ground cumin, dried oregano, and bay leaf. Stir well to combine.
    - Bring the mixture to a boil, then reduce the heat and simmer uncovered for about 1-1.5 hours, or until the pork is tender and the flavors have melded together. Stir occasionally, and add more chicken broth if needed to maintain the desired consistency.
    - Season with salt and freshly ground black pepper to taste.
4. **Serve:**
    - Remove the bay leaf before serving.
    - Serve the Puerco en Salsa Verde with warm tortillas, or alongside rice and beans.
    - Garnish with sliced radishes, chopped fresh cilantro, and lime wedges.

Tips:

- **For Extra Flavor:** Add a few tablespoons of the leftover salsa verde to the finished dish for added brightness.
- **Adjusting Heat:** If you prefer a milder dish, use fewer jalapeños or remove the seeds before roasting.
- **Make-Ahead:** This dish can be prepared ahead of time and stored in the refrigerator for up to 3 days. It also freezes well for up to 3 months.

Enjoy your delicious Puerco en Salsa Verde!

www.ingramcontent.com/pod-product-compliance
Lightning Source LLC
LaVergne TN
LVHW081603060526
838201LV00054B/2043